11+
Verbal Reaso
GL & Other Styles

TESTBOOK **2**

Standard 20 Minute Tests

Dr Stephen C Curran
with Warren Vokes
Edited by Andrea Richardson

This book belongs to

Accelerated Education Publications Ltd

A B C D E F G H I J K L M N O P Q R S T U V W X Y Z

Verbal Reasoning Test 1

1) Underline the word which does not fit in with the others.

   pane   tumbler   straw   bottle   <u>porthole</u>

2) If **12345** means **DREAM**, then **42531** means ___armed___ .

3) What is the ninth letter of the alphabet? (__I__)

4) Write the next two letters in this series.

   C   G   K   O   __S__   __W__

5) The same three letters occur in all five words below. Make a word from them.

   BRACED   TARMAC   CRATER   CREATE   TREACLE   (__arc__)

6) In the sentence below, five consecutive letters spell a number. Write this number, as a word, inside the brackets.

   It was a warm summer's <u>evening</u> and the sky was clear.   (__seven__)

7) Make a word from the letters which remain after the word **GIANTS** has been made from the letters of the two words **TAGS** and **FAINT**. (__sat__)

8) Underline the word which would come first if these words were arranged in alphabetical order.

   clump   <u>clamber</u>   climber   clamp   cloud

9) Inside the brackets write the letter which will end the first word and begin the second.

   SOL (__O__) **NLY**

10) Insert the missing word which continues this word pattern.

    creed, reed   clump, lump   chide, __hide__

11) Inside the brackets write the four-letter word which will complete all five words.

    ____man   ____bin   ____cart   ____pan   ____less (_____)

A B C D E F G H I J K L M N O P Q R S T U V W X Y Z

12) Write the word which has both these meanings.
    (a) a fox's tail
    (b) a tool with bristles and a handle (_brush_)

13) Complete this analogy:

    Left is to **right** as **west** is to _east_

14) Underline the word below which can be made from some or all of the letters of the word **CONSERVATORY**, using each letter not more than once.

    RASH   TREE   SOME   TRAY   SURE

15) Rearrange the letters of the word in capitals to form a word corresponding to the meaning given.

    TABS: flying nocturnal mammals (_bats_)

16) Inside the brackets, write the word of four letters needed to complete the unfinished word.

    The smoke from the cannon could be seen long before we heard the re _____ . (_____)

17) In a certain code **CFIHO** means **TEACH**.
    What does **HOFIC** mean in the same code? (_cheat_)

18) Insert the word which will complete the sentence and rhymes with the word in capital letters.

    RATE: Angela checked her _weight_ on the bathroom scales.

19) Underline the two words below which are most opposite in meaning.

    happy   mean   rude   generous   stout   angry

20) In the space provided, write the missing word formed by rearranging the letters of the word in heavy type.

    Although his **knee** hurt, Alex was _keen_ to finish the charity walk.

Score [ ]   Percentage [ ] %

A B C D E F G H I J K L M N O P Q R S T U V W X Y Z

Verbal Reasoning Test 2

1) Which letter is eighth from the end of the alphabet? (_____)

2) Insert the missing word which continues this word pattern.

   boar, board   grin, grind   crow, _____

3) In the space provided, write the missing word formed by rearranging the letters of the word in heavy type.

   He **drove** into the car park and his eyes _____ around looking for a space.

4) The same three letters occur in all five words below. Make a word from them.

   TAPING   PLINTH   TRIPLE   TYPIST   IMPORT (_____)

5) Inside the brackets write the letter which will end the first word and begin the second.

   SHU (_____) EEN

6) In a certain code **VBOCQM** means **WARNED**.
   What would **WANDERER** be in the same code?   (_____)

7) Inside the brackets write the three-letter word which will complete all five words.

   ____loft   ____rick   ____stack   ____ride   ____wire (_____)

8) Underline the two words below which are similar in meaning.

   steer   row   drift   moor   glide   sink

9) Write the word which has both these meanings.
   (a) short beard growth on a man's face
   (b) short stalks in a field after harvesting   (_____)

10) Underline the two words which should change places in order to make this sentence correct.

    The satellite transmits the Earth and orbits signals to the tracking station.

A B C D E F G H I J K L M N O P Q R S T U V W X Y Z

11) Inside the brackets, write the word of five letters needed to complete the unfinished word.

   Miners work _____ ground in deep tunnels.   (_____)

12) Complete this analogy: **White** : **black** as **north** : _____

13) If **53124** means **HEART**, then _____ means **THEATRE**.

14) Write the next two letters in this series.

   V   S   P   M   ____   ____

15) Underline the word which cannot be made from some or all of the letters of the word **EXTRAORDINARY**, using each letter not more than once.

   ERRAND   ROTARY   ADORN   ANOREXIA   ROUND

16) Underline the word which does not fit in with the others.

   stork   duck   swan   goose   flamingo   sparrow

17) Underline the word which is opposite in meaning to the word in capitals.

   MINIMAL: negligible   most   token   slight   least

18) Underline the word which would come last if these words were arranged in alphabetical order.

   mediocre   mendacity   mentor   medicine   mention

19) Complete this analogy by underlining one word from each set of brackets.

   Length is to (metre, ruler, width) as **depth** is to (fathom, submarine, ocean)

20) In the sentence below, five consecutive letters spell the name of a relative. Write this word inside the brackets.   (_____)

   The boys had fun cleaning the old coins and seeing them shine again.

Score [ ]   Percentage [ ]%

A B C D E F G H I J K L M N O P Q R S T U V W X Y Z

Verbal Reasoning Test 3

1) Inside the brackets write the four-letter word which will complete all five words.

   ____ key   ____ over   ____ pike   ____ spit   ____ coat   (_____)

2) Insert the missing word which continues this word pattern.

   best, test   waste, taste   roast, _____

3) Complete this analogy: **Train** is to **track** as **boat** is to _____

4) In the sentence below, five consecutive letters spell the name of a vessel. Write this word inside the brackets.

   He wound the line round the bollard on the mooring.   (_____)

5) Make a word from the letters which remain after the word **PLACE** has been made from the letters of the two words **CATCH** and **LEAP**.

   (_____)

6) If **143254** means **RENAME**, then **542341** means _____ .

7) Underline the word which is most similar in meaning to the word in capitals.

   REPEAL: abolish   build   enact   reduce   enforce

8) How many more consonants than vowels are there in the word **IRRETRIEVABLY**?   (_____)

9) Write the next two terms in this letter series.

   AZ   DW   GT   JQ   _____   _____

10) Underline the word which cannot be made from some or all of the letters of the word **IMPOSSIBLE**, using each letter not more than once.

    SIMILES   MISSILES   EMBOSS   SPIES   BESOM

11) Insert the word which will complete the sentence and rhymes with the word in capital letters.

    RUDE: He _____ all his own beer at home.

A B C D E F G H I J K L M N O P Q R S T U V W X Y Z

12) Underline the word which does not fit in with the others.

    car   bus   tram   bicycle   lorry   motorcycle

13) Rearrange the letters of the word in capitals to form a word corresponding to the meaning given.

    TIDE: to prepare a text for publication by correcting errors and ensuring clarity and accuracy   (_____)

14) Underline the two words below which are most opposite in meaning.

    dirty   heavy   easy   smelly   musty   onerous

15) Underline the word which would come third if these words were arranged in alphabetical order.

    denounce   denegrate   denude   deny   denominate

16) Write the word which has both these meanings.
(a) to be opposed or express opposition to something
(b) something visible and tangible   (_____)

17) The same four letters occur in all five words below. Make a word from them.

    PLANTED TRAMPLE CAPTURE DEPART TRAIPSE (_____)

18) Underline the word which cannot be made from some or all of the letters of the word **IRRESISTIBLE**, using each letter not more than once.

    RISIBLE   LIBERTIES   STYLES   TRILBIES   REBELS

19) Inside the brackets, write the four-letter word needed to complete the unfinished word.

    Colin held back his friend to pre_____ him stepping into the road. (_____)

20) Underline the two words which should change places in order to make this sentence correct.

    The car showed when the traffic lights stopped red.

Score [ ] Percentage [ ] %

A B C D E F G H I J K L M N O P Q R S T U V W X Y Z

Verbal Reasoning Test 4

1) In the sentence below, three consecutive letters spell the name of a unit of currency. Write this word inside the brackets.

   There were hardly enough sandwiches to feed everyone. (_____)

2) Write the word which has both these meanings.
   (a) to pester somebody
   (b) a burrowing animal   (_____)

3) Which letter of the alphabet comes immediately before the third vowel? (___)

4) Inside the brackets write the letter which will end the first word and begin the second.

   CLA (_____) **ROD**

5) Inside the brackets write the four-letter word which will complete all five words.

   ____ cast   ____ done   ____ flow   ____ leaf   ____ hang   (_____)

6) Insert the word which will complete the sentence and rhymes with the word in capital letters.

   JOY: The ship kept well clear of the _____ that marked the wreck.

7) Make a word from the letters that remain after the word **SPRAIN** has been made from the letters of the two words **TRAIN** and **PASS**.   (_____)

8) In the space provided, write the missing word formed by rearranging the letters of the word in heavy type.

   The boys **raced** to the _____ tree and back.

9) Arrange these words in alphabetical order by numbering them 1-5:

   groundless (__) greatness (__) grizzle (__) greedily (__) gruesome (__)

10) Underline the word which does not fit in with the others.

    elm   oak   ash   chestnut   rhododendron   sycamore

A B C D E F G H I J K L M N O P Q R S T U V W X Y Z

11) If **92746** means **PENAL**, then _____ means **PLANE**.

12) Inside the brackets, write the word of six letters needed to complete the unfinished word.

   He gave the shopkeeper the money and the trans _____ was completed.

   (_____)

13) Underline the word which cannot be made from some or all of the letters of the word **CIRCUMNAVIGATE**, using each letter not more than once.

   CAVING   CURATIVE   MAGICIAN   ACUMEN   VACUUM

14) Notice how the second word of each pair has been formed from the first, then write the missing word.

   lace, brace   light, bright   levity, _____

15) The same three letters occur in all five words below. Make a word from them.

   TIEPIN   CONCEPT   EMPATHY   TEMPORAL   KETCHUP (_____)

16) Rearrange the letters of the word in capitals to form a word corresponding to the meaning given.

   LEAP: lacking colour or intensity   (_____)

17) Insert the missing word that continues this word pattern.

   car, cart   for, fort   tor, _____

18) Underline the word that is opposite in meaning to the word in capitals.

   TINY: small   enormous   little   grand   obese

19) Complete this analogy: **Flavour** is to **taste** as **odour** is to _____

20) Write the next two terms in this letter series.

   PM   **QL**   **RK**   **SJ**   _____   _____

Score [ ]   Percentage [ ]%

A B C D E F G H I J K L M N O P Q R S T U V W X Y Z

Verbal Reasoning Test 5

1) The word **ASLEEP** in a certain code is **BTMFFQ**.
   What would the word **ACTIVE** be in the same code?   (_____)

2) Write the next two terms in this letter series.

   DL   EM   FN   GO   _____   _____

3) In the sentence below, five consecutive letters spell the name of a fruit.
   Write this word inside the brackets.

   The poor little chap pleaded with her to wait for him catch up. (_____)

4) Rearrange the first four letters of the word **SKIRMISH** so they form a word.
   (_____)

5) Rearrange the letters of the word in capitals to form a word that completes the sentence.

   PLEAD: The _____ fell off and he could cycle no further.

6) Inside the brackets, write the word of four letters needed to complete the unfinished word.

   The prim _____ is a small perennial plant with colourful flowers. (_____)

7) If the first three vowels were omitted from the alphabet, what would the ninth letter be?   (_____)

8) Underline the word which cannot be made from some or all of the letters of the word **INVIGILATE**, using each letter not more than once.

   AGILE   GIVING   ALIEN   INVITE   ENTAIL

9) Complete this analogy: **Lamb** is to **sheep** as **leveret** is to _____

10) Write the three consecutive letters in the word **POSTURES** which are also consecutive in the alphabet.   (_____)

A B C D E F G H I J K L M N O P Q R S T U V W X Y Z

11) Insert the missing word which continues this word pattern.

    grate, gate   shame, same   spend, _____

12) Is the following statement true or false?

    A kilogram of water weighs more than a kilogram of petrol.   (_____)

13) Underline the word which does not fit in with the others.

    copper   zinc   lead   iron   steel   gold

14) Insert the word which will complete the sentence and rhymes with the word in capital letters.

    SEIZE: Josie ate fish and chips with mushy _____ .

15) Underline the two words which should change places in order to make this sentence correct.

    He put some loose change so he found it in the collection bucket.

16) Underline the word which is similar in meaning to the word in capitals.

    RAPTURE: burst   depression   glee   elation   melancholy

17) Inside the brackets write the letter which will end the first word and begin the second.

    STA (_____) **ANCH**

18) Write the word which has both these meanings.
    (a) the location where somebody lives
    (b) a formal speech or report   (_____)

19) If **624315** means **CANDLE**, then **124653** means _____ .

20) Inside the brackets write the five-letter word which will complete all five words.

    ____ line   ____ dog   ____ hand   ____ lay   ____ mine   (_____)

Score [ ] Percentage [ ] %

A B C D E F G H I J K L M N O P Q R S T U V W X Y Z

Verbal Reasoning Test 6

1) Insert the missing word which continues this word pattern.

   pail, rail   pack, rack   pole, _____

2) Rearrange the letters of the word in capitals to form a word corresponding to the meaning given.

   START: pies that have no crust top   (_____)

3) Underline the two words which should change places in order to make this sentence correct.

   He won the car at a blistering pace and drove the race.

4) Underline the word which is most opposite in meaning to the word in capitals.

   MUSCULAR: strong   puny   heavy   burly

5) If **341621** means **PLEASE**, then _____ means **ELAPSE**.

6) Insert the word which will complete the sentence and rhymes with the word in capital letters.

   PLEASED: The customs officials _____ the contraband.

7) In the space provided, write the missing word formed by rearranging the letters of the word in heavy type.

   Thieves **steal** valuable _____ tiles from the roofs of buildings.

8) Write the vowels which come between **F** and **V** in the alphabet. (_____)

9) Rearrange the last six letters of the word **MELODIC** so they form a word.
   (_____)

10) Complete this analogy: **Eye** is to **sight** as **ear** is to _____

11) Notice how the second word of each pair has been formed from the first, then write the missing word.

   tiles, stile   takes, stake   tones, _____

12
© 2012 Stephen Curran

A B C D E F G H I J K L M N O P Q R S T U V W X Y Z

12) In a certain code **ZBLTVOW** means **PARENTS**.
    What would **TVOLBZW** stand for in the same code? (_____)

13) Inside the brackets write the letter which will end the first word and begin the second.
    STOR (___) ATCH

14) Underline the word which cannot be made from some or all of the letters of the word **PROFESSIONALS**, using each letter not more than once.
    SENIORS   FLORINS   REFINES   PERSONAL   SENSOR

15) Inside the brackets, write the word of three letters needed to complete the unfinished word.
    A ___ quet is an elaborate meal attended by many guests. (_____)

16) Write the next two terms in this letter series.
    CD   HI   MN   RS   _____   _____

17) Underline the two words below which are similar in meaning.
    rap   speak   knock   shout   whisper   whistle

18) Make a word from the letters which remain after the word **ATOMS** has been made from the letters of the two words **BOAT** and **SMUG**.
    (_____)

19) Inside the brackets write the four-letter word which will complete all five words.
    ____hill   ____load   ____time   ____size   ____fall   (_____)

20) If you think the following statement is true write T, if false write F.
    The year **20 BC** came after the year **19 BC**. (___)

Score ___ Percentage ___%

A B C D E F G H I J K L M N O P Q R S T U V W X Y Z

Verbal Reasoning Test 7

1) Write the word which has both these meanings.
   (a) an award for a winner
   (b) to lever something open (_____)

2) Is this statement true or false?

   The year **1937** came in the second half of the twentieth century. (_____)

3) Inside the brackets, write the word of six letters needed to complete the unfinished word.

   The plans were drawn by an expert _____ man. (_____)

4) In the sentence below, six consecutive letters spell the name of a type of bird. Write this word inside the brackets.

   He could damage his health rushing around like that. (_____)

5) Make a word from the letters which remain after the word **CONSENTS** has been made from the letters of the two words **TENNIS** and **SOCCER**. (_____)

6) Write the three consecutive letters in the word **OVERSTAY** which are also consecutive in the alphabet. (_____)

7) In a certain code **PWVSOW** stands for **STRAIT**.
   What would the word **ARTIST** be in the same code? (_____)

8) Inside the brackets write the letter which will end the first word and begin the second.
   BRO (_____) **IND**

9) Underline the word which does not fit in with the others.

   honey   treacle   syrup   sugar   lemon   saccharin

10) Rearrange the letters of the word in capitals to form a word which completes the sentence.

    INAPT: She set up her easel and prepared to _____ his portrait.

A B C D E F G H I J K L M N O P Q R S T U V W X Y Z

11) Underline the word which is similar in meaning to the word in capitals.

   DIRE: awful   colourful   grim   wonderful   deadly

12) Underline the two words which should change places in order to make this sentence correct.

   A fiery audience congregated to hear the politician's hushed speech.

13) Underline the word which cannot be made from some or all of the letters of the word **EMULATES**, using each letter not more than once.

   TEAM   SLATE   STEAM   MEETS   SALUTES

14) If **2463517** means **SEABIRD** then **3165247** means _____ .

15) Underline the two words below which are most opposite in meaning.

   tame   gaudy   ripe   round   mild   dull

16) Insert the missing word which continues this word pattern.

   moat, meat   bloat, bleat   groat, _____

17) Write the next two terms in this letter series.

   AE   **FJ**   **KO**   **PT**   _____   _____

18) Rearrange the letters of the word in capitals to form a word corresponding to the meaning given.

   SWEAT: use something carelessly   (_____)

19) Insert the word which will complete the sentence and rhymes with the word in capital letters.

   HURT: Malik squeezed hard and managed to _____ the last of the toothpaste out of the tube.

20) Notice how the second word of each pair has been formed from the first, then write the missing word.

   ploughed, plough   slowed, slow   quashed, _____

Score ☐   Percentage ☐ %

A B C D E F G H I J K L M N O P Q R S T U V W X Y Z

Verbal Reasoning Test 8

1) Write in alphabetical order the consonants in the word **UNFATHOMABLE**

   (_____)

2) Write the word which has both these meanings.
   (a) a financial penalty for wrong doing
   (b) when everything is going well   (_____)

3) Underline the word which cannot be made from some or all of the letters of the word **SPECIMEN**, using each letter not more than once.

   PENS   NIECE   PIECE   MICE   SPENT

4) In the space provided, write the missing word formed by rearranging the letters of the word in heavy type.

   They had to stay in the community **centre** after the _____ floods.

5) Underline the two words below which are most similar in meaning.

   long   durable   inexpensive   tall   fast   tough

6) Underline the two words which should change places in order to make this sentence correct.

   Jasmine fished three perch when she caught the river.

7) In the sentence below, five consecutive letters spell a word meaning an alloy of iron and carbon. Write this word inside the brackets.

   His department was charged with maximising waste elimination. (_____)

8) Insert the missing word which continues this word pattern.

   sprout, pot   assign, sin   upland, _____

9) Move one letter from the first word and place it into the second word to make two new words. Write the two new words in the spaces provided.

   CHEAP and **LAMP** = _____ and _____

10) Write the next two terms in this letter series.

    SD   TE   VG   YJ   _____   _____

A B C D E F G H I J K L M N O P Q R S T U V W X Y Z

11) Underline the word which does not fit in with the others.

    bolster   pillow   quilt   bed   duvet   blanket

12) Underline the word which is most opposite in meaning to the word in capitals.

    COMPLIANT: upset   dirty   amenable   compatible   defiant

13) Complete this analogy: **Pound** is to **kilo** as _____ is to **metre**

14) If **95726** means **RENTS**, then _____ means **STERN**.

15) Inside the brackets, write the word of five letters needed to complete the unfinished word.

    A _____ let is an item of jewellery worn round the wrist.   (_____)

16) Notice how the second word of each pair has been formed from the first, then write the missing word.

    barber, rear   villas, sail   ostler, _____

17) In a certain code **LWKEA** stands for **JUICY**.
    What word does the code **INQCV** stand for?   (_____)

18) The same three letters occur in all five words below. Make two different three-letter words from them.

    CANOPY   PATERNITY   MANPOWER   PAINLESS   RAPIDNESS

    (_____ and _____)

19) Rearrange the letters of the word in capitals to form a word corresponding to the meaning given.

    PAINTER: to relate or have relevance to something   (_____)

20) Inside the brackets write the word which rhymes with the word in capitals and corresponds to the meaning given.

    SLOW: a mixture of flour and water   (_____)

Score [ ]   Percentage [ ]%

© 2012 Stephen Curran

A B C D E F G H I J K L M N O P Q R S T U V W X Y Z

Verbal Reasoning Test 9

1) Notice how the second word of each pair has been formed from the first, then write the missing word.

   stile, tile   shack, hack   small, _____

2) Underline the word which cannot be made from some or all of the letters of the word **EVENTUALLY** using each letter not more than once.

   VALLEY   LEVEL   VENUE   AUNTY   ADVENT

3) Insert the word which will complete the sentence and rhymes with the word in capital letters.

   REEF: The _____ appeared in court charged with stealing a car.

4) Which letter of the alphabet comes immediately after the third vowel? (____)

5) Inside the brackets write the letter which will end the first word and begin the second.

   COM (____) OAT

6) Underline the two words below which are similar in meaning.

   complain   annoy   shout   point   irritate   cry

7) Underline the two words which should change places in order to make this sentence correct.

   The old flood water swept the rushing man off his feet.

8) Rearrange the letters of the word **BEARD** so as to form a word meaning:

   excluded somebody from taking part   (_____)

9) Underline the two words below which are most opposite in meaning.

   save   respect   talk   die   contempt   sleep

10) Write the word which has both these meanings.
    (a) to transmit electricity
    (b) the way a person behaves   (_____)

A B C D E F G H I J K L M N O P Q R S T U V W X Y Z

11) Make a word from the letters which remain after the word **BOASTFUL** has been made from the letters of the two words **CONFUSES** and **TABLE**.

(_____)

12) Notice how the second word of each pair has been formed from the first, then write the missing word.

diary, dry　　　squad, sad　　　falsely, _____

13) Underline the word which does not fit in with the others.

shawl　　jumper　　cardigan　　shirt　　trousers　　jacket

14) In the space provided, write the missing word formed by rearranging the letters of the word in heavy type.

The noise from the engine _____ to a damaged **piston**.

15) Make a word by rearranging the three consecutive letters in the word **SELFDEFENSIVE** which are also consecutive in the alphabet. (_____)

16) Complete this analogy:

Cent is to **dollar** as **pence** is to _____

17) In the sentence below, four consecutive letters spell the name of a part of the human anatomy. Write this word inside the brackets.

"Please wash, starch and iron my shirt ready for tomorrow." (_____)

18) Write the vowels which come in the first half of the alphabet.　　(_____)

19) Inside the brackets write the five-letter word which will complete all five words.

out _____　sun _____　shoe _____　star _____　moon _____　(_____)

20) Which letter occurs twice in the words **REPENTANT** and **STATEMENT**, but not at all in the word **QUICKLY**?

(_____)

Score ☐　Percentage ☐ %

A B C D E F G H I J K L M N O P Q R S T U V W X Y Z

Verbal Reasoning Test 10

1) Underline the two words which should change places in order to make this sentence correct.

   The horse lowed softly and the cows whinnied in reply.

2) Write the vowels contained in the word **LONGITUDINAL** in alphabetical order. (_____)

3) Notice how the second word of each pair has been formed from the first, then write the missing word.

   wobble, we   onion, on   usurp, _____

4) Underline the word which is most similar in meaning to the word in capitals.

   WAYWARD: compliant   haughty   disobedient   lengthy   happy

5) Underline the word which cannot be made from some or all of the letters of the word **TREPIDATION**, using each letter not more than once.

   PRIDE   PATTERN   DRAIN   PREDICTION   RATION

6) Rearrange the letters of the word in capitals to form a word corresponding to the meaning given.

   SOLEMN: round, juicy gourd fruit   (_____)

7) Make a word from the letters which occur only once in the word **PARAPHRASED**. (_____)

8) In the space provided, write the missing word formed by rearranging the letters of the word in heavy type.

   A strong **gust** of wind _____ the tent peg out of the ground.

9) Notice how the second word of each pair has been formed from the first, then write the missing word.

   punnet, put   dairy, day   genial, _____

10) In a certain code **EJTDFSO** stands for **DISCERN**.
    What would **GLIMPSE** be in the same code? (_____)

20   © 2012 Stephen Curran

A B C D E F G H I J K L M N O P Q R S T U V W X Y Z

11) Underline the word below which cannot be made from some or all of the letters of the word **INTERCONTINENTAL**, using each letter not more than once.

    ANCIENT   CLIENTELE   CLARINET   RETENTION   INNOCENT

12) Complete this analogy:

    Pink is to **red** as _____ is to **black**

13) Inside the brackets write the three-letter word which will complete all five words.

    ____ less   ____ ion   ____ work   ____ ally   ____ room   (_____)

14) Rearrange the second, fifth, eighth, ninth and twelfth letters of the word **INADVERSITIES** so they form a word.

    (_____)

15) Inside the brackets write two letters which will end the first word and begin the second.

    AMORO (_____) **EABLE**

16) Underline the word which does not fit in with the others.

    steam   cloud   water   condense   oil   dew

17) In a certain code **QPETX** means **REACT**.
What would **TQEXP** stand for in the same code?   (_____)

18) Inside the brackets, write the word of four letters needed to complete the unfinished word.

    The claivoyant claimed she could fore____ the future.   (_____)

19) Underline the two words below which are most opposite in meaning.

    final   fat   deceased   jolly   alive   kind

20) The same three letters occur in all five words below. Make a word from them.

    POLUTION PLUNDER NUPTIALS JUNIPER UNPOLISHED (_____)

Score   Percentage   %

© 2012 Stephen Curran

A B C D E F G H I J K L M N O P Q R S T U V W X Y Z

Verbal Reasoning Test 11

1) Write the word which has both these meanings.
   (a) a unit of currency
   (b) to repeatedly hit something with force   (_____)

2) Underline the word which cannot be made from some or all of the letters of the word **MATHEMATICS**, using each letter not more than once.

   SMITE   ASTHMA   HAMMERS   EMITS   CHEMIST

3) If the letters of the alphabet were numbered **1, 2, 3, 4, 5** etc., what word would the letters numbered **13, 9, 19, 5, 18, 25** spell?   (_____)

4) Underline the two words below which can be made from some or all of the letters of the word **NOMENCLATURE**, using each letter not more than once.

   NUANCE   ENCOUNTERS   LACES   ORNAMENT   ELECTORAL

5) Underline the word which is most similar in meaning to the word in capitals.
   CHARISMATIC: handsome   captivating   popular   talkative   sad

6) In the sentence below, six consecutive letters spell the name of a handtool. Write this word inside the brackets.

   Buying a franchise let him start a business in which he was self-employed.

   (_____)

7) Inside the brackets write two letters which will end the first word and begin the second.
   STRI (_____) **NCE**

8) Write the three consecutive letters in the word **PHONOPHOBIA** which are also consecutive in the alphabet.   (_____)

9) Arrange these words in alphabetical order by numbering them 1-5:

   room (___)   roam (___)   rouble (___)   rocky (___)   rotunda (___)

10) Underline the two words which should change places in order to make this sentence correct.

    It is easier to descend up a ladder than to climb.

A B C D E F G H I J K L M N O P Q R S T U V W X Y Z

11) Rearrange these letters to spell one of the seasons: **WNIRET**   (_____)

12) Rearrange the letters of the word in capitals to form a word corresponding to the meaning given.

   TREADLE: changed   (_____)

13) Inside the brackets write the three-letter word which will complete all five words.

   ____hole   ____band   ____rest   ____lock   ____chair   (_____)

14) Inside the brackets write the same two letters which will end the first word and begin the second word in both sets of words.

   HOU (____) RVE

   VER (____) TEE

15) Which letter occurs once in the word **SETTLED**, twice in **COSSETED** but not at all in **HOTELIER**?   (_____)

16) The same three letters occur in all five words below. Make a word from them.

   CENTENARY   COURTYARD   HEARTY   REALLY   YEARLY (_____)

17) Make a word from the letters which remain after the words **CANAL** and **LIPS** have been made from the letters of the word **RAPSCALLION**.   (_____)

18) Rearrange the capital letters below to form a word corresponding to the meaning given.

   ANCHI: found on a bicycle   (_____)

19) Insert the word which will complete the sentence and rhymes with the word in capital letters.

   CHOSE: He lacked sleep but felt much more alert after a short _____ .

20) If the code for **CART** is **BZQS**, what is the code for **DESK**?   (_____)

Score [   ]   Percentage [   ]%

A B C D E F G H I J K L M N O P Q R S T U V W X Y Z

Verbal Reasoning Test 12

1) Insert the missing word which continues this word pattern.

   drawer, reward   desserts, stressed   deliver, _____

2) Rearrange the letters of the word in capitals to form a word corresponding to the meaning given.

   AMBER: a freshwater fish   (_____)

3) In the sentence below, six consecutive letters spell the name of a Christmas decoration. Write this word inside the brackets.

   Waste bins were put in selected locations to reduce litter.   (_____)

4) In a certain code **BZOTWCXVM** means **STREAMING**. What would **TCXMOWVZB** stand for in the same code?

   (_____)

5) Underline the two words which should change places in order to make this sentence correct.

   Spain and Greece are many destinations for popular holidaymakers.

6) Underline the word below which can be made from some or all of the letters of the word **STREAMLINED**, using each letter not more than once.

   DISMANTLED   MISLEADING   DERAILMENTS   MASTERS   TENTS

7) If **24687531** means **ORGANIST** then _____ means **ROASTING**.

8) Write the next two terms in this letter series.

   TC   **NE**   **IH**   **EL**   _____   _____

9) Underline the two words below which are most opposite in meaning.

   dischord   enemy   loyal   harmony   rapture

10) In the space provided, write the missing word formed by rearranging the letters of the word in heavy type.

    Canoeists have to **master** the strong currents found in a fast _____.

A B C D E F G H I J K L M N O P Q R S T U V W X Y Z

11) Make a word of four letters from the letters which occur twice in the word **DONATION**. (_____)

12) All the words below are in alphabetical order except one. Underline this word.

    extent   external   extreme   extoll   extract

13) Underline the word which does not fit in with the others.

    swim   run   walk   trot   hop   jog

14) Write the word of four letters which completes the unfinished word and corresponds to the meaning given.

    a deep blue precious stone   sapp_____

15) Underline the word which cannot be made from some or all of the letters of the word **TUBERCULOSIS**, using each letter not more than once.

    BLISS   CURLS   CUTE   CRISIS   SLUICE

16) Inside the brackets write the four-letter word which will complete all five words.

    ____ book   ____ over   ____ brake   ____ rail   ____ some (_____)

17) Insert the word which will complete the sentence and rhymes with the word in capital letters.

    COME: The dentist's injection made his face feel completely _____ .

18) Underline the word which is most similar in meaning to the word in capitals.

    DEARTH: glut   infertile   width   plenty   lack

19) Complete the sentence below by writing the same seven-letter word in both spaces.

    He wrapped the _____ and gave it to his sister when all her friends were _____ at her birthday party.

20) The same three letters occur in all five words below. Make a word from them.

    SOLICITOR HOSTILE POLICE SOLUTION DOCILE   (_____)

Score ☐ Percentage ☐ %

© 2012 Stephen Curran

A B C D E F G H I J K L M N O P Q R S T U V W X Y Z

Verbal Reasoning Test 13

1) Inside the brackets write the two-letter word which will complete all five words.

   __activity   __capable   __admissible   __come   __digestible   (_____)

2) Write the next two terms in this letter series.

   AF   **ZH**   **BJ**   **YL**   _____   _____

3) Notice how the second word of each pair has been formed from the first, then write the missing word.

   release, lease   stutter, utter   elicit, _____

4) In the car park, the Volvo is on the left of the Nissan and the BMW is parked on the left of Volvo. Which car is parked in the middle? (_____)

5) The same two letters in the same order will complete all six words below. Write these letters inside the brackets.

   r__d   s__k   t__d   c__l   l__d   f__l   (_____)

6) Complete the sentence below by writing the same word in both spaces.
   To stop the bleeding, the paramedic _____ a bandage around his arm to cover the _____ .

7) These two rows of squares represent two words. The letters in the first row of squares are the same as those directly below them. Study the clues, then write the words.

   ☐☐ ☐   a baby's bed
   ☐☐☐☐   a item of winter clothing

8) In a certain code **XTV** means **PAN** and **OCD** means **SIT**.
   What would **XCVDO** mean in the same code?   (_____)

9) One word from the five on the left can be joined to one word from the five on the right to form a compound word. Underline the two words.

   (high, dry, under, on, low)   (off, to, cold, heat, wet)

10) Which is the fourteenth consonant in the alphabet?   (_____)

26   © 2012 Stephen Curran

A B C D E F G H I J K L M N O P Q R S T U V W X Y Z

11) Underline the word which does not fit in with the others.

   duckling   piglet   foal   bull   calf

12) If **1437256** means **GLISTEN**, then **2361457** means _____ .

13) Underline the two words which should change places in order to make this sentence correct.

   Peter had grown new so he needed a taller pair of trousers.

14) In the sentence below, seven consecutive letters spell the name of an occupation. Write this word inside the brackets.

   Put each error behind you and call it experience!   (_____)

15) Inside the brackets write the word which rhymes with the word in capitals and corresponds to the meaning given.

   COW: a farming tool to turn over the soil   (_____)

16) In the space provided, write the missing word formed by rearranging the letters of the word in heavy type.

   He was awarded two _____ for helping a **damsel** in distress.

17) These two rows of squares represent two words. The letters in the lower squares are the same as those directly above them. Study the clues, then complete the words.

   a fold in a pair of trousers or a skirt   C ☐ ☐ S ☐
   to stop, or to end   C ☐ ☐ S ☐

18) Underline the word which is most similar in meaning to the word in capitals.

   BENEVOLENT: brutal   heartless   angry   dangerous   kind

19) Underline the word which cannot be made from some or all of the letters of the word **VICEROY**, using each letter not more than once.

   COVER   RICE   RIVER   VOICE   VERY

20) Make a word from the letters that remain after the word **AERATOR** has been made from the letters of the two words **TAILOR** and **LATER**.

   (_____)

Score ☐   Percentage ☐ %

A B C D E F G H I J K L M N O P Q R S T U V W X Y Z

Verbal Reasoning Test 14

1) Inside the brackets, write two letters which will end the first word and begin the second.

   DRA (_____) RBS

2) Underline the word which would come in the middle if these words were arranged in alphabetical order.

   brain   breast   bread   bridle   brooch

3) How many more consonants than vowels are there in the word **TRANSFIGURATION**? (_____)

4) Rearrange the middle four letters of the word **MARINADE** so they form a word. (_____)

5) Insert the word which will complete the sentence and rhymes with the word in capital letters.

   PEWS: The comedian's jokes failed to _____ the audience.

6) Inside the brackets, write the word of four letters needed to complete the unfinished word.

   The charity increased its funds after the recent ap_____ .   (_____)

7) If **CRIME** in code is **3 18 9 13 5**, then **VICTOR** in code is _____ .

8) Underline the word which would come in the middle if the words below were arranged to form a sentence.

   exercise maintain will health Daily help good physical to

9) Underline the word below which is most similar in meaning to a person who shows sympathy.

   affable   compassionate   duplicitous   heartless   charismatic

10) Observe how the words inside the brackets have been formed in the two examples given, then complete the missing word.

    W(AL)K   T(AL)L   D(_____)E

28   © 2012 Stephen Curran

A B C D E F G H I J K L M N O P Q R S T U V W X Y Z

11) If **STEAMER** in code is **YCBMTBW**, then the code **TBCWBY** means _____ .

12) In the space provided, write the missing word formed by rearranging the letters of the word in heavy type.

   The **premise** that _____ have always been replaced with democratic governments is flawed.

13) Using all the letters of the word **ORNITHOLOGIST** only once, three other words were made. If two of the words were **SIGHT** and **ROOT**, what was the other word?   (_____)

14) Below is a line from a crossword puzzle together with its clue. Complete the word by writing one letter only in each blank square.

   | S | E | | | I | | E | | covered in small, shiny clothing decorations.

15) Underline the word which is most similar in meaning to the word in capitals.

   INSOLVENT: puzzled   hidden   bankrupt   violent   unresolved

16) Underline the word which is the odd one out.

   robin   thrush   starling   pigeon   tit   hawk

17) Write the word which has both these meanings.
    (a) to knock or tip something over
    (b) to make somebody unhappy   (_____)

18) The four words on the left are alike in some way. One word on the right also has this likeness. Underline this word.

   (trip, train, tulip, travel)   (brain, strut, trial, rip)

19) Underline the word which cannot be made from some or all of the letters of the word **PECULIAR**, using each letter not more than once.

   CLIP   RIPE   CLEAR   RAIL   RECALL

20) The same three letters occur in all five words below. Make a word from them.

   NOBILITY   BANISH   BRAINY   BRINY   OBSTINATE   (_____)

Score ☐   Percentage ☐ %

© 2012 Stephen Curran

A B C D E F G H I J K L M N O P Q R S T U V W X Y Z

Verbal Reasoning Test 15

1) Underline the word which does not fit in with the others.

   London   Birmingham   Manchester   Glasgow   Liverpool

2) Make a word from the letters which remain after the words **AIR** and **AT** have been made from the letters of the word **IMPARTIAL**.   (_____)

3) The same two letters in the same order will complete all six words below. Write these letters inside the brackets.

   s__t   c__d   w__e   p__t   f__k   b__n   (_____)

4) Underline the two words below which are similar in meaning.

   divide   replace   take   remove   multiply

5) In the sentence below, four consecutive letters spell the name of an kitchen appliance. Write this word inside the brackets.

   I love not having to wear my school uniform.   (_____)

6) Which letter comes immediately before the last vowel in the alphabet? (____)

7) These two rows of squares represent two words. The letters in the lower squares are the same as those directly above them. Study the clues, then write the words.

   a payment to use property

   a rank in the army

8) Insert the missing word which continues this word pattern.

   eat, beats   one, bones   awl, _____

9) If **52431** means **TEARS**, then **15432** means _____ .

10) Inside the brackets write the four-letter word which will complete all five words.

    ____black   ____tree   ____box   ____maker   ____shine   (_____)

11) The second word below is made by rearranging the letters of the first word. Rearrange the letters of the third word in the same way to find the missing word.

    LEAD : DEAL :: READ : _____

A B C D E F G H I J K L M N O P Q R S T U V W X Y Z

12) Underline the two words which should change places in order to make this well known saying correct.

   A bird in the hand is bush two in the worth.

13) If **RED** in code is **CWE** and **HAT** is **OPZ**, what is **THREAD** in the same code? (_____)

14) Rearrange the letters of the word in capitals to form a word corresponding to the meaning given.

   SLATE: small freshwater ducks (_____)

15) Inside the brackets, write the word that rhymes with the word in capital letters and corresponds with the meaning given.

   OUT: a long period of extremely dry weather (_____)

16) Complete the sentence below by writing the same word in both spaces.

   She jumped with a _____ when the pistol fired for the _____ of the race.

17) Below is a line from a crossword puzzle together with its clue. Complete the word by writing one letter only in each blank square.

   ☐ E ☐ ☐ S A R ☐   essential

18) Observe how the word inside the brackets has been formed in the example given, then write the missing word.

   GRIEVE (OGRE) ONCE   OCEANS (_____) RANK

19) Underline the word below which cannot be made from some or all of the letters of the word **GREENHOUSE**, using each letter not more than once.

   SERENE   GROUSE   ONEROUS   ROUGHEN   HEROES

20) One word from the five on the left can be joined to one word from the five on the right to form a compound word. Underline the two words.

   (arm, head, leg, foot, body)   (glove, hat, blouse, belt, dress)

Score ☐   Percentage ☐ %

A B C D E F G H I J K L M N O P Q R S T U V W X Y Z

Verbal Reasoning Test 16

1) Inside the brackets write two letters which will end the first word and begin the second.

    CRA (_____) **ASE**

2) Below is a line from a crossword puzzle together with its clue. Complete the word by writing one letter only in each blank square.

    | E | | | I | | I | | O | | somebody with work on display

3) Underline the word which would come last if the words below were arranged to form a sentence.

    a telephone creates Answering the good impression politely

4) If **CAUSE** in code is **73481**, then _____ is **834718**.

5) Observe how the word inside the brackets has been formed in the example given, then write the missing word.

    BRAVE (BONE) DRONE   TAPER (_____) ALIEN

6) Underline the word which would come fourth if these words were arranged in alphabetical order.

    quoit   quell   quip   quaff   queue   quarrel

7) Complete this analogy: **Aunt** is to **uncle** as _____ is to **nephew**

8) In the sentence below, six consecutive letters spell the name of a root vegetable. Write this word inside the brackets.

    He acquired the camera dishonestly by stealing it from the shop.

                                                                                 (_____)

9) If four days after tomorrow is Tuesday, what was the day before yesterday?   (_____)

10) Rearrange the two middle letters and the last two letters of the word **CANTANKEROUS** so they form a word.   (_____)

11) If these words were written backwards, underline the word which would come in the middle if they were then arranged in alphabetical order.

    asked   limped   replied   sound   hummed

A B C D E F G H I J K L M N O P Q R S T U V W X Y Z

12) If **PULSATE** in code is **SXOVDWH**, then **JUDICIAL** is _____.

13) Underline the word which cannot be made from some or all of the letters of the word **AEROPLANE**, using each letter not more than once.

   PEOPLE   APRON   OPENER   REPEAL   ENROL

14) Insert the word which will complete the sentence and rhymes with the word in capital letters.

   RAINED: Sehdev _____ injury to avoid the cross country run.

15) These two rows of squares represent two words. The letters in the lower squares are the same as those directly above them. Study the clues, then write the words.

   ☐☐☐☐☐ to move sideways
   ☐☐☐☐   lazy and unwilling to work

16) Using all the letters of the word **SATELLITES** only once, three other words were made. If two of the words were **SEA** and **SIT**, what was the other word?

   (_____)

17) Complete this analogy by underlining one word from each set of brackets.

   Perfume is to (bottle, nose, neck, canvas) as **palate** is to (brush, meal, easel, mouth)

18) Underline the two words below which are most opposite in meaning.

   robust   prickly   sticky   fragile   metallic   noisy

19) Inside the brackets, write the word of four letters needed to complete the unfinished word.

   The musicians in the (_____)stand were sheltered from the rain.

20) Underline the word which does not fit in with the others.

   mushroom   truffle   yeast   flour   toadstool   mould

Score ☐   Percentage ☐ %

A B C D E F G H I J K L M N O P Q R S T U V W X Y Z

Verbal Reasoning Test 17

1) Underline the word below which cannot be made from some or all of the letters of the word **SUBVERSION**, using each letter not more than once.

   ENVIOUS   REVISION   NERVOUS   ISSUE   NOISE

2) Below is a line from a crossword puzzle together with its clue. Complete the word by writing one letter only in each blank square.

   ☐ ☐ V I ☐ E   relating or belonging to the genus of ruminant animals that includes cattle, oxen, and buffalo.

3) Claire's birthday is two months after Sophia's. Sophia's birthday is in the month whose third letter is the 16th letter of the alphabet. In what month was Claire born?   (_____)

4) If **9173658** stands for **PARSLEY**, what does **7596183** stand for?   (_____)

5) If Natsuki observes the sun rising in Tokyo, her shadow would be cast to the:

   NORTH   SOUTH   EAST   WEST   (_____)

6) One word from the five on the left can be joined to one word from the five on the right to form a compound word. Underline the two words.

   (beef, pork, chicken, ham, veal)   (rope, twine, yarn, thread, string)

7) Write all the consonants of the word **TRANSCENDENTALISM** in alphabetical order.   (_____)

8) Write the next two terms in this letter series.

   DW   EV   GU   JT   _____   _____

9) Inside the brackets write the four-letter word which will complete all five words.

   ____ray   ____age   ____hole   ____able   ____ions   (_____)

10) Rearrange the capital letters below to form a word corresponding to the meaning given.

    EGGHAL: to try to settle on a price   (_____)

34   © 2012 Stephen Curran

A B C D E F G H I J K L M N O P Q R S T U V W X Y Z

11) Insert the missing word which continues this word pattern.

   pill, pail   hill, hail   till, _____

12) If **SUPERSTITIOUS** in a code is **VWCAPVXBXBEIV**, then the codes for **PURSUIT** and **TOURIST** will be _____ and _____.

13) Underline the word which is most similar in meaning to the word in capitals.

   LANGUISH: thrive   stiffen   deteriorate   rest   mope

14) Complete the sentence below by writing the same word in both spaces.

   No-one remembered the _____ but _____ still, even his wife failed to recognize him after so many years absence.

15) Underline the word which does not fit in with the others.

   mound   groove   furrow   trench   ditch

16) These two rows of squares represent two words. The letters in the lower squares are the same as those directly above them. Study the clues, then write the words.

   ☐☐☐☐☐☐ to lose something temporarily
   ☐☐ ☐   ☐   lightly flavoured

17) Insert the word which will complete the sentence and rhymes with the word in capital letters.

   KITE: The windfarm is a _____ on the landscape.

18) In the sentence below, seven consecutive letters spell the name of a large ocean-going vessel. Write this word inside the brackets.

   The ship was sailing so close to Manhattan Island he could almost taste America.   (_____)

19) Make a word from the letters which remain after the word **PERPETUAL** has been made from the letters of the three words **BULGE**, **PILE** and **TRAP**.

   (_____)

20) Underline the word which is the odd one out.

   colonel   major   sergeant   bosun   corporal

Score ☐   Percentage ☐ %

© 2012 Stephen Curran

A B C D E F G H I J K L M N O P Q R S T U V W X Y Z

Verbal Reasoning Test 18

1) One word from the five on the left can be joined to one word from the five on the right to form a compound word. Underline the two words.

   (light, torch, lack, deep, large)   (shine, candle, bread, lustre, cross)

2) In the space provided, write the missing word formed by rearranging the letters of the word in heavy type.

   She hated snakes and had a **dread** that she would step on an _____ .

3) Underline the word which cannot be made from some or all of the letters of the word **VOLATILE**, using each letter not more than once.

   VIOLATE   OLIVE   TAILOR   VALET   ATOLL

4) The four words on the left are alike in some way. One word on the right also has this likeness. Underline this word.

   (static, sense, erratic, cool)   (open, crash, beggar, moving)

5) Underline the word which is the odd one out.

   disorder   riot   picnic   disturbance   confusion   violence

6) The same four letters occur in both the words **RANCOROUS** and **CHASTEN**. Make two four-letter words from them.   (_____ and _____)

7) Underline the word which would come in the middle if these words were arranged in alphabetical order.

   generate   genial   general   genteel   gentry

8) The same three letters occur in all five words below. Make a word from them.

   NEPOTISM   PIMIENTOS   JUNIPER   PRESENT   PREVENT (_____)

9) Insert the word which will complete the sentence and rhymes with the word in capital letters.

   SHEIKH: He was late to bed and found it hard to _____ up next morning.

10) Using all the letters of the word **GRATEFUL** only once, two other words were made. If one of the words was **FLAG**, what was the other word?   (_____)

36   © 2012 Stephen Curran

A B C D E F G H I J K L M N O P Q R S T U V W X Y Z

11) Complete this sentence by inserting the word with the opposite meaning of the word in heavy type.

   Although only a few minutes previously the situation was _____, suddenly it had become **critical**.

12) If **TRAMLINE** in code is **18437296**, then **TERMINAL** in the same code is _____ .

13) Observe how the word inside the brackets has been formed in the example given, then write the missing word.

   RANCH (CHAPS) GASP   LURCH (_____) DIET

14) These two rows of squares represent two words. The letters in the first row of squares are the same as those directly below them. Study the clues, then write the words.

   ☐ ☐☐☐ to cook food in an oven
   ☐☐☐☐ to slow down or stop

15) In a certain code **TGYCTFU** means **REWARDS**.
   What does **RGPCNVA** mean in the same code?   (_____)

16) Inside the brackets, write the word of four letters needed to complete the unfinished word.

   The _____ heads in the Titanic failed and the ship sank.   (_____)

17) Underline the two words inside the brackets which go best with the two words in capitals.

   COLD : DRY   (warm, wet, humid, hot, stifling, damp)

18) Underline the word which describes someone who has no fixed abode.

   destitute   dangerous   hapless   itinerant   sanguine

19) Write the word which has both these meanings.
   (a) a raised shelf or ridge
   (b) an establishment that deals with money   (_____)

20) The second word below is made by rearranging the letters of the first word. Rearrange the letters of the third word in the same way to find the missing word.

   PEAL : LEAP :: FOAL : _____

Score ☐   Percentage ☐ %

A B C D E F G H I J K L M N O P Q R S T U V W X Y Z

Verbal Reasoning Test 19

1) Inside the brackets write two letters which will end the first word and begin the second.

   WOR (_____) ILL

2) Write the word which has both these meanings.
   (a) the answer to a puzzle
   (b) a fluid with a substance dissolved in it   (_____)

3) Write in capitals the letter which comes 12th from the end of the alphabet. (____)

4) The same four letters occur in all five words below. Make a word from them.

   DOCKER   DRACONIAN   DECORATE   RECOVERED   CROWNED
   (_____)

5) Notice how the second word of each pair has been formed from the first, then write the missing word.

   blasts, last   stakes, take   usurer, _____

6) Underline the word which does not fit in with the others.

   prostrate   helpless   exhausted   strong   impotent

7) Inside the brackets, write the word that rhymes with the word in capitals and corresponds to the meaning given.

   TIPPED: an underground room, often below a church   (_____)

8) Write three words of four letters which can be made from the first six letters of the word **IMPROVEMENT**, using each letter not more than once in each word.
   (_____ and _____ and _____)

9) One word from the four on the left can be joined to one word from the four on the right to form a compound word. Underline the two words.

   (shift, death, back, tool)   (in, stage, move, crown)

10) All the words below are in alphabetical order except one. Underline this word.

    treachery   treacle   treadle   treasurer   treason

38   © 2012 Stephen Curran

A B C D E F G H I J K L M N O P Q R S T U V W X Y Z

11) These two rows of squares represent two words. The letters in the lower squares are the same as those directly above them. Study the clues, then write the words.

   to supply something ☐☐☐☐☐☐

   a source of personal satisfaction ☐☐ ☐☐☐

12) The second word below is formed by rearranging the letters of the first word. Rearrange the letters of the third word in the same way to find the missing word.

   DENT: TEND :: PROD : _____

13) If **SWEAT** in a code is **BSPTC**, then **BCPS** means:

   EAST   WEST   SEAT   SWAT   STEW   (_____)

14) Underline the two words inside the brackets which go best with the two words in capitals.

   PIT : MOUNTAIN   (weight, depth, mass, height, breadth)

15) Complete this analogy: **Pebble** is to **boulder** as **twig** is to _____

16) Underline the word which describes a person who is devious.

   arrogant   resourceful   loud   cunning   friendly

17) In the sentence below, six consecutive letters describe a rural, privately owned property with a large residence. Write this word inside the brackets.

   The biggest ate the most food and grew larger than the rest.   (_____)

18) Observe how the words inside the brackets have been formed in the two examples given, then complete the missing word.

   B(ON)D   B(ON)E   P(____)Y

19) Make a word from the letters which remain after the word **EVOLUTION** has been made from the letters of the two words **OVULATE** and **IRONY**.

   (_____)

20) In the space provided, write the missing word formed by rearranging the letters of the word in heavy type.

   Her forearm was very swollen **below** her _____ where the bee had stung her.

Score ☐   Percentage ☐ %

A B C D E F G H I J K L M N O P Q R S T U V W X Y Z

Verbal Reasoning Test 20

1) Underline the word which does not fit in with the others.

   lord   minion   manager   boss   leader   chief

2) Rearrange the letters of the word in capitals to form a word corresponding to the meaning given.

   RETRIAL: a short advertisement for a film   (_____)

3) Insert the missing word which continues this word pattern.

   cure, curse   gore, gorse   pure, _____

4) The same four letters occur in all five words below. Make two different words from them.

   DISTURB   STUDIOUS   TRUSSED   TRUNDLES   DOUBTS

   (_____ and _____)

5) If the code for **SHRIVEL** is **RTCBWFZ**, then the codes for **VEIL** and **RISE** will be:

   ZBWF   RBCF   CBZF   WFBZ   TFCR   CBRF

   (_____ and _____)

6) Below is a line from a crossword puzzle together with its clue. Complete the word by writing one letter only in each blank square.

   ☐ D ☐ R ☐ ☐ O ☐   great love and esteem

7) Inside the brackets write two letters which will end the first word and begin the second.

   RESI (_____) **MAND**

8) Move one letter from the first word and place it into the second word to make two new words. Write the two new words in the spaces provided.

   PRANG and **CANE** = _____ and _____

9) One word from the four on the left can be joined to one word from the four on the right to form a compound word. Underline the two words.

   (rip, cut, tear, slit)   (round, down, out, up)

10) Write the next two letters in this series.

    T   Q   O   L   J   ____   ____

40   © 2012 Stephen Curran

A B C D E F G H I J K L M N O P Q R S T U V W X Y Z

11) Complete this analogy: Eagle : talon as tiger : _____

12) Prianka and Sally like fried eggs. Tom and Tandip like boiled eggs. Sally and Tom like poached eggs. Who likes both poached and fried eggs?   (_____)

13) The four words on the left are alike in some way. One word on the right also has this likeness. Underline this word.

   (toner, honest, lonely, throne)   (whole, tune, money, thrift)

14) Insert the word which will complete the sentence and rhymes with the word in capital letters.

   CUFF: She struggled to answer the _____ question.

15) These two rows of squares represent two words. The letters in the first row of squares are the same as those directly below them. Study the clues, then write the words.

   to lose brightness, colour or loudness gradually
   the front of a building

16) Underline the word which is opposite in meaning to the word in capitals.

   SOMNOLENT: noisy   alert   hungry   tiresome   ringing

17) Underline the two words which should change places in order to make this well known saying correct.

   There's a crock of rainbow at the end of this gold.

18) Observe how the word inside the brackets has been formed in the example given, then write the missing word.

   CHARM (STARE) STEER   FINER (_____) TOADY

19) Rearrange the middle four letters of the word **DESPATCHED** so they form a word.   (_____)

20) Complete the sentence below by writing the same word in both spaces.

   He was _____ to exhaustion but he knew he must not _____ his eyes or he would fall sound asleep and succumb to exposure.

Score ___   Percentage ___ %

A B C D E F G H I J K L M N O P Q R S T U V W X Y Z

Verbal Reasoning Test 21

1) If **9 16 13 7 11 15 2** in code means **CANTERS**, then
   7 15 16 13 9 11 2 in the same code means _____ .

2) Move one letter from the first word and place it into the second word to make two new words. Write the two new words in the spaces provided.

   POISE and **FEND** = _____ and _____

3) Write the next two terms in this letter series.

   ET   GR   IP   KN   ____   ____

4) Inside the brackets, write the four-letter word which will complete all four words.

   loop____   pot____   key____   peep____   pin____   (_____)

5) If **LIVER** is **JGTCP** in code, what is **RMLESC** as a word?

   (_____)

6) Underline the word which does not fit in with the others.

   dissent   differ   combine   protest   separate   disagree

7) In the sentence below, five consecutive letters spell the name of a colour. Write this word inside the brackets.

   I am bereft of all hope since my son's death.   (_____)

8) Below is a line from a crossword puzzle together with its clue. Complete the word by writing one letter only in each blank square.

   | I | F | □ | □ | U | □ | having an extremely bad reputation

9) The second word below is made by rearranging the letters of the first word. Rearrange the letters of the third word in the same way to find the missing word.

   LUMP : PLUM :: IDEA : _____

10) Underline the two words below which are similar in meaning.

    wail   heave   twist   relax   lug

A B C D E F G H I J K L M N O P Q R S T U V W X Y Z

11) Notice how the second word of each pair has been formed from the first, then write the mising word.

   bread, dare   Midas, said   valet, _____

12) If all the vowels were removed from the alphabet, which letter would then be the fifteenth?   (_____)

13) Underline the word which is the odd one out.

   cot   nappy   bib   rusk   abacus   rattle

14) In the space provided, write the missing word formed by rearranging the letters of the word in heavy type.

   To **rustle** cattle is illegal and will _____ in arrest.

15) These two rows of squares represent two words. The letters in the first row of squares are the same as those directly below them. Study the clues, then write the words.

   ☐ ☐☐   ☐   pulled by a horse
   ☐☐☐☐☐☐☐   a woodwind instrument

16) Make a word from the letters which remain after the word **PLEASANT** has been made from the letters of the three words **SNAP**, **PLACE** and **ROT**.   (_____)

17) Complete the sentence below by writing the same word in both spaces.

   She hoped the goverment department would _____ her request and award her a _____ towards the cost of her education.

18) Rearrange the letters of the word in capitals to form a word corresponding to the meaning given.

   GLARE: a light coloured beer   (_____)

19) Underline the word below which can be made from some or all of the letters of the word **FUSILLADE**, using each letter not more than once.

   FUSSED   DEALT   DELUDE   FLAILED   FLUTED

20) Underline the two words which should change places in order to make this sentence correct.

   Use the weight to measure the scales of the ingredients.

Score ☐   Percentage ☐ %

A B C D E F G H I J K L M N O P Q R S T U V W X Y Z

Verbal Reasoning Test 22

1) If **264135** means **CONKER**, then **532164** means _____ .

2) Rearrange the middle six letters of the word **INTERMINABLE** so they form a word. (_____)

3) Underline the two words inside the brackets which go best with the two words in capitals.

   SNAIL : CRAB   (cockle, starfish, oyster, plankton, slug, butterfly)

4) In the space provided, write the missing word formed by rearranging the letters of the word in heavy type.

   Four ornate **piers** supported a church steeple topped with a _____ .

5) Which letters occur in the word **ASSASSINATED**, but not in the word **TASTE**? Make a word from these letters. (_____)

6) Underline the word which would come last if the words below were arranged to form a sentence.

   generosity depend on Charities to others people's help

7) Arrange these words in alphabetical order by numbering them 1-5:

   bureau (___)   butter (___)   buttress (___)   butane (___)   butcher (___)

8) Underline the word which does not fit in with the others.

   cheesecake   gateaux   pâté   mousse   pavlova   crumble

9) Complete this analogy: **Drum** is to **beat** as **flute** is to _____

10) Using all the letters of the word **VOCIFEROUSLY** only once, three other words were made. If two of the words were **SOUR** and **VOICE**, what was the other word? (_____)

11) If **RADIO** in code is **SCGMT**, then the code **SJBQJ** means _____ .

44   © 2012 Stephen Curran

A B C D E F G H I J K L M N O P Q R S T U V W X Y Z

12) Underline the word which describes sound that is unpleasantly loud.

   subdued   raucous   bawdy   melodious   rhythmic

13) The four words on the left are alike in some way. One word on the right also has this likeness. Underline this word.

   (wrap, quack, balm, deign)   (rope, gnat, leave, pain)

14) Rearrange the capital letters below to form a word which completes the sentence.

   MNIRFUO: The soldier went on parade in his _____ .

15) In the space provided, write the missing word formed by rearranging the letters of the word in heavy type.

   The accident was **crass** stupidity and he still bears the _____ of his injury.

16) Below is a line from a crossword puzzle together with its clue. Complete the word by writing one letter only in each blank square.

   ☐ A ☐ ☐ I ☐ H   to become dull and discoloured.

17) Inside the brackets, write the word of six letters needed to complete the unfinished word.

   The Bayeaux tapestry is a great attr _____ for visitors to France.

18) Underline the word which cannot be made from some or all of the letters of the word **REPLENISH** using each letter not more than once.

   RELISH   SPHERES   HELPERS   REPELS   RINSE

19) Observe how the word inside the brackets has been formed in the example given, then write the missing word.

   PRIDE (PARE) BLADE   BLAME (_____) CREST

20) One word from the five on the left can be joined to one word from the five on the right to form a compound word. Underline the two words.

   (neck, shin, toe, elbow, leg)   (stair, slide, sill, pace, cap)

Score ☐   Percentage ☐ %

A B C D E F G H I J K L M N O P Q R S T U V W X Y Z

Verbal Reasoning Test 23

1) Underline the word which is the group name for each of the others.

    orangutan   chimpanzee   gibbon   ape   gorilla   bonobo

2) Insert the missing word which continues this word pattern.

    buck, cask   luck, mask   suck, _____

3) In the space provided, write the missing word formed by rearranging the letters of the word in heavy type.

    The body's immune system may _____ to just a **trace** of allergens.

4) Rearrange the letters of the word in capitals to form a word corresponding to the meaning given.

    WREATHE: state of the atmosphere   (_____)

5) Underline the odd one out.

    motion   shimmer   flow   movement   activity

6) If **6423157** means **CHORALS**, then **7642513** means _____ .

7) Underline the two words which should change places in order to make this sentence correct.

    Sir Alexander Fleming discovered the penicillin agent in antibacterial.

8) Complete the sentence below by writing the same word in both spaces.

    A _____ in his character lead him to _____ and spy for the enemy.

9) Inside the brackets write the two-letter word which will complete all five words.

    ____ sure   ____ step   ____ side   ____ sane   ____ sect   (_____)

10) Observe how the words inside the brackets have been formed in the two examples given, then write the missing word.

    B(BARK)K   D(DART)T   C(_____)E

11) In the sentence below, six consecutive letters spell the name of a weapon. Write this word inside the brackets.

    When he double checked his oilcan none was left.   (_____)

46   © 2012 Stephen Curran

A B C D E F G H I J K L M N O P Q R S T U V W X Y Z

12) Underline the word below which can be made from some or all of the letters of the word **PNEUMONIA**, using each letter not more than once.

   POUND   PIANOS   MEANT   INANE   MINUTE

13) If **PWERVU** stands for **TRAVEL** and **XEPCYX** stands for **NATION**, what does **RCYUVXP** stand for?   (_____)

14) These two rows of squares represent two words. The letters in the first row of squares are the same as those directly below them. Study the clues, then write the words.

   □□   □   to take to the air
   □□□□□□   decorated with floral designs

15) Write the next two terms in this letter series.

   GHI   **FGH**   **EFG**   **DEF**   _____   _____

16) Inside the brackets write the word which rhymes with the word in capitals and corresponds to the meaning given.

   PRAYED: a length of entwined hair   (_____)

17) One word from the five on the left can be joined to one word from the five on the right to form a compound word. Underline the two words.

   (under, cross, round, drive, steer)   (turn, winch, pull, wind, twist)

18) Make a word from the letters which remain after the word **PETUNIAS** has been made from the letters of the three words **PAIN**, **POSE** and **TOUR**.
   (_____)

19) Below is a line from a crossword puzzle together with its clue. Complete the word by writing one letter only in each blank square.

   □□□L□F□   to become eligible

20) If **QRPYU** means **STRAW**, then **CHIDE** in code is:

   EJKFG   AFGBC   AFGAC   EJKFH   AFJBC   (_____)

Score ☐   Percentage ☐ %

A B C D E F G H I J K L M N O P Q R S T U V W X Y Z

Verbal Reasoning Test 24

1) Underline the two words inside the brackets which go best with the two words in capitals.

   TILLER : **MAST** (sailing, hull, keel, yacht, wind)

2) If the code for **FRUIT** is **BPUKX**, what is the code for **JUICE**?

   (_____)

3) In the sentence below, five consecutive letters spell the name of a unit of volume. Write this word inside the brackets.

   In winter the fire was lit regardless of the temperature.   (_____)

4) Using all the letters of the word **ATTENUATE** only once, two other words were made. If one of the words was **EATEN**, what was the other word?   (_____)

5) Inside the brackets write two letters which will end the first word and begin the second.

   LIQU (_____) **ANGE**

6) If **TIGER** in code is **21 10 8 6 19**, then **LEOPARD** in code is

   _____ .

7) These two rows of squares represent two words. The letters in the first row of squares are the same as those directly below them. Study the clues, then write the words.

   ☐☐☐☐   a stringed instrument
   ☐☐☐☐☐☐☐   a barbed spear with a rope attached

8) Underline the word which would come seventh if the words below were arranged to form a sentence.

   England left all drives traffic In the road on

9) Below is a line from a crossword puzzle together with its clue. Complete the word by writing one letter only in each blank square.

   ☐ L ☐ ☐ H ☐ D   dressed

10) Which consonant in the word **ATHEISM** is nearest to the third vowel?   (___)

A B C D E F G H I J K L M N O P Q R S T U V W X Y Z

11) Insert the word which will complete the sentence and rhymes with the word in capital letters.

   POUND: She ingested too much water and _____ .

12) Underline the two words below which are most opposite in meaning.

   pessimistic   ravenous   affluent   morose   cheerful

13) If **AYQFGCP** means **CASHIER**, then **NYWKCLR** means _____ .

14) One word from the five on the left can be joined to one word from the five on the right to form a compound word. Underline the two words.

   (road, rail, track, trail, way)   (ticket, fare, journey, timetable, return)

15) Underline the word which is the odd one out.

   Paraguay   Columbia   Mexico   Peru   Chile

16) Underline the word which would come in the middle if these words were arranged in alphabetical order.

   drain   drudgery   draconian   dross   dreadful

17) Observe how the word inside the brackets has been formed in the example given, then write the missing word.

   STRUT (REST) EAST   TRAYS (_____) CAST

18) Inside the brackets, write the four-letter word needed to complete the unfinished word.

   The Black Death was a pes____nce that raged across Europe. (_____)

19) In the space provided, write the missing word formed by rearranging the letters of the word in heavy type.

   To **reclaim** wasteland and build Britain's Olympic Park was a modern engineering _____ .

20) Underline the word which cannot be made from some or all of the letters of the word **LACERATION**, using each letter not more than once.

   ARCANE   RAINCOAT   OCARINA   CRANIAL   CAUTION

Score [   ]   Percentage [   ]%

A B C D E F G H I J K L M N O P Q R S T U V W X Y Z

Verbal Reasoning Test 25

1) Write the next two terms in this letter series.

   GI   HF   IC   _____   _____

2) Underline the word which is the odd one out.

   sure   resolved   unlikely   fixed   decided   indisputable

3) Rearrange the letters of the word in capitals to form a word corresponding to the meaning given.

   SCALPS: small buckles or fastenings   (_____)

4) Complete the sentence below by writing the same word in both spaces.

   The dustman's lorry was so full he had to _____ any more _____ .

5) Below is a line from a crossword puzzle together with its clue. Complete the word by writing one letter only in each blank square.

   D E ☐ ☐ N T   deliberately disobedient

6) Make a word, which begins with **P**, from the letters which remain after the word **SALTWATER** has been made from the letters of the three words **PLANET**, **STAR** and **WIDE**.   (_____)

7) Observe how the word inside the brackets has been formed in the example given, then write the missing word.

   OCHRE (STORM) MOST   PANIC (_____) DATE

8) Underline the two words which should change places in order to make this sentence correct.

   The car squealed as the tyres cornered at high speed.

9) If **VEO** means **LOT** and **ZTVW** means **RELY**, how would **TROLLEY** be written in the same code?   (_____)

10) In the space provided, write the missing word formed by rearranging the letters of the word in heavy type.

    The boy had to **study** in a _____ old library.

50   © 2012 Stephen Curran

A B C D E F G H I J K L M N O P Q R S T U V W X Y Z

11) Underline the two words below which are similar in meaning.

    occlude   break   uncover   block   exclude   open

12) The same two letters in the same order will complete all five words below. Write these letters inside the brackets.

    l__e   t__e   s__up   g__o   p__e   (_____)

13) **RESULT** in code is **SGVYQZ**. What would **QTRHZIA** mean in the same code? (_____)

14) Underline the word which does not fit in with the others.

    lottery   win   chance   bet   wager   gamble

15) Inside the brackets write the six-letter word which will complete all five words.

    ___ power   ___ stick   ___ light   ___ snuffer   ___ wick (_____)

16) In the sentence below, five consecutive letters spell the word which means a hauling or lifting device. Write this word inside the brackets.

    Kelly was determined to win championship medals in swimming.

                                                                          (_____)

17) The second word below is formed by rearranging the letters of the first word. Rearrange the letters of the third word in the same way to find the missing word.

    STEP : PEST :: SHAM : _____

18) Underline the word which cannot be made from some or all of the letters of the word **FRAUDULENT**, using each letter not more than once.

    FEUDAL   TREACLE   TEARFUL   FLAUNT   UNFURLED

19) One word from the five on the left can be joined to one word from the five on the right to form a compound word. Underline the two words.

    (near, far, just, blow, only)   (snow, ice, rain, mud, frost)

20) Notice how the second word of each pair has been formed from the first, then write the missing word.

    masticate, mate   regular, rear   difference, _____

Score [ ]   Percentage [ ] %

A B C D E F G H I J K L M N O P Q R S T U V W X Y Z

Verbal Reasoning Test 26

1) The four words on the left are alike in some way. One word on the right also has this likeness. Underline this word.

   (screw, crow, sacred, cruise)   (turn, skill, crack, score)

2) Underline the word which is the group name for each of the others.

   profession   theatre   law   accountancy   medicine   science

3) Four days after tomorrow is Sunday. What day was three days before yesterday?   (_____)

4) Notice how the second word of each pair has been formed from the first, then write the missing word.

   dictator, dictates   dilution, dilutes   relative, _____

5) Below is a line from a crossword puzzle together with its clue. Complete the word by writing one letter only in each blank square.

   | L | _ | _ | I | _ | A | _ | well thought out

6) One word from the five on the left can be joined to one word from the five on the right to form a compound word. Underline the two words.

   (fire, ash, smoke, flame, heat)   (stack, pile, mound, dump, heap)

7) If **VOLATILE** in code is **WNMZUHMD**, what would **UDNOPQBK** mean in the same code?   (_____)

8) Complete this analogy:

   Sheep is to **bleat** as **snake** is to _____

9) Arrange these words in alphabetical order by numbering them 1-5:

   tragic (__)   transmit (__)   traffic (__)   tricky (__)   trellis (__)

10) Underline the word which describes something that is extremely poisonous infectious, or damaging to organisms.

    bellicose   malicious   virulent   unpleasant   odious

11) Rearrange the ninth, seventh, fifth, second and first letters of the word **MEDICATION** so they form a word.   (_____)

52   © 2012 Stephen Curran

A B C D E F G H I J K L M N O P Q R S T U V W X Y Z

12) If **GEYSER** in code is **9 7 1 21 7 20**, then **16 17 20 6 11 5** is _____ .

13) These two rows of squares represent two words. The letters in the first row of squares are the same as those directly below them. Study the clues, then write the words.

    ☐ ☐☐☐   a tiresome and demanding selfish child
    ☐☐☐☐☐☐   to scold somebody vigorously and lengthily

14) Insert the word which will complete the sentence and rhymes with the word in capital letters.

    TALE: A white_____ covered the bride's face during the marriage.

15) Observe how the word inside the brackets has been formed in the example given, then write the missing word.

    STONE (SCENT) CRUET   ARMED (_____) NUDGE

16) Write the word which has both these meanings.
    (a) to make something more confusing
    (b) a mass of particles of water in the sky   (_____)

17) Using all the letters of the word **BINOCULARS** only once, three other words were made. If two of the words were **SOUL** and **IN**, what was the other word?   (_____)

18) Complete this sentence by inserting the word with the opposite meaning of the word in heavy type.

    We should not be **deceitful** but _____ and truthful at all times.

19) The same four letters occur in all five words below. Make two different words from them.

    NUMERAL   ENTRAILS   ALERTS   NEUTRAL   LATRINES
                                        (_____ and _____)

20) In the space provided, write the missing word formed by rearranging the letters of the word in heavy type.

    Either cover your **heads** or stay in the _____ out of the sun.

Score ☐ Percentage ☐ %

A B C D E F G H I J K L M N O P Q R S T U V W X Y Z

Verbal Reasoning Test 27

1) These two rows of squares represent two words. The letters in the first row of squares are the same as those directly below them. Study the clues, then write the words.

   ☐☐☐☐☐   a gnat-like insect
   ☐☐☐☐☐☐   a very small person

2) Write the vowels which come between **F** and **Q** in the alphabet. (_____)

3) Underline the word which does not fit in with the others.

   regret   rue   repent   grieve   celebrate   sorrow

4) Inside the brackets write the four-letter word which will complete all five words.

   ___ land   ___ sick   ___ less   ___ spun   ___ stead   (_____)

5) If **XAVOK** means **MUSIC** and **VZBEAY** means **SPROUT**, what does **VKBAXZYOEAV** mean in the same code?

   (_____)

6) In the space provided, write the missing word formed by rearranging the letters of the word in heavy type.

   The decorator would **bristle** if someone suggested the paint would

   _____ if not applied properly.

7) Inside the brackets write the word which rhymes with the word in capitals and corresponds to the meaning given.

   RAFTS: a board game played with counters.   (_____)

8) Underline the word which is similar in meaning to the word in capitals.

   AGGRAVATE: improve   measure   weigh   soothe   worsen   remedy

9) One word from the five on the left can be joined to one word from the five on the right to form a compound word. Underline these two words.

   (cycle, truck, cart, barrow, lorry)   (van, car, bell, wheel, base)

10) If **KPXVF** means **FLUTE** then **GEQLP** means _____ .

11) Underline the word which does not fit in with the others.

    gap   continuity   space   interval   break   hiatus

54   © 2012 Stephen Curran

A B C D E F G H I J K L M N O P Q R S T U V W X Y Z

12) In the sentence below, five consecutive letters spell the word that describes where metal is heated and shaped. Write this word inside the brackets.

It is easy for germs to spread on dirty surfaces. (_____)

13) The same two letters in the same order will complete all five words below. Write these letters inside the brackets.

wh__k   d__l   s__f   b__t   h__m   (_____)

14) Make a word from the letters which remain after the word **MOSAIC** has been made from the letters of the three words **COSY**, **PIE** and **MAT**. (_____)

15) Notice how the second word of each pair has been formed from the first, then write the missing word.

facilitate, fate   bellow, blow   locate, _____

16) Underline the word which would come fifth if the words below were arranged to form a well-known saying.

that gold glitters is not All

17) If **FOURTH** in code is **ULFIGS**, what is **EIGHTH** in the same code? (_____)

18) Underline the word below which can be made from some or all of the letters of the word **ADULTERATE**, using each letter not more than once.

ALTERS   TAUTEN   MUTTER   ALERTED   LEADEN

19) Rearrange the capital letters below to form a word corresponding to the meaning given.

VAILAS: liquid secreted into the mouth   (_____)

20) Observe how the word inside the brackets has been formed in the example given, then write the missing word.

RAGES (SUGAR) AUGER   EXCEL (_____) EASES

Score ____   Percentage ____%

© 2012 Stephen Curran   55

A B C D E F G H I J K L M N O P Q R S T U V W X Y Z

Verbal Reasoning Test 28

1) In the space provided, write the missing word formed by rearranging the letters of the word in heavy type.

   The **plates** in the dinner service were decorated with _____ .

2) Three of the four words below are given in code. The codes are not written in the same order as the words and one code is missing.

   CONE   TEAM   BONE   BENT   9726   8625   5643

   a) Find the code for **BACON**.   (_____)
   b) Find the word for **362496**.   (_____)

3) In the space provided, write the missing word formed by rearranging the letters of the word in heavy type.

   I _____ to buy some **tinned** fruit today to keep in my cupboard.

4) These two rows of squares represent two words. The letters in the first row of squares are the same as those directly below them. Study the clues, then write the words.

   ☐☐   ☐☐   a humped animal
   ☐☐☐☐☐☐   a soft toffee made with sugar

5) Which two letters in the word **JOCULARITY** come between the 3rd and 4th vowels of the alphabet?   (_____)

6) Underline the word which cannot be made from some or all of the letters of the word **TEMPERAMENTAL**, using each letter not more than once.

   METRE   TAMPER   REALM   TRAMPLE   MELTED

7) If **FRAME** in code is **UIZNV**, what does **XFIGZRM** mean in the same code?   (_____)

8) In this question there are three pairs of words. Complete the third pair in the same way as the first two pairs. Write the new word in the space provided.

   (letters, lets)   (pillage, pale)   (soonest, ____)   (_____)

9) Underline the word which describes a strong feeling of dislike.

   deprivation   partiality   desertion   aversion   penchant

10) Below is a line from a crossword puzzle together with its clue. Complete the word by writing one letter only in each blank square.

    ☐☐B L☐T☐   the innards of an edible fowl

A B C D E F G H I J K L M N O P Q R S T U V W X Y Z

11) Inside the brackets write two letters which will end the first word and begin the second.

          VER (_____) NSE

12) Rearrange the capital letters below to form a word which completes the sentence.

    ALCEER: Every morning we have _____ with milk and sugar.

13) In the sentence below, six consecutive letters spell the name of a fuel. Write this word inside the brackets.

    Sandie seldom visited the cinema with her friends.   (_____)

14) Underline the word which would come last if these words were arranged in alphabetical order.

    screech   scruffy   scramble   scruples   scrounge

15) Write the word which has both these meanings.
    (a) to fascinate
    (b) to cast a spell on somebody   (_____)

16) Underline the two words which would come in the middle if the words below were arranged to form a sentence.

    light objects make of heavy Levers moving work

17) Using all the letters of the word **SWEETHEART** only once, three other words were made. If two of the words were **SET** and **HE**, what was the other word?   (_____)

18) Underline the word which is the odd one out.

    group   crowd   assembly   meeting   gathering   solitude

19) In the sentence below, the word in capital letters has had three consecutive letters taken out. These three letters will make one correctly spelt word without changing their order. Write this word inside the brackets.

    RERIATE is to send someone back to their country of birth.   (_____)

20) The same four letters occur in all four words below. Make a word from them.

    TRUSTING   GROUTING   TROUNCES   GRUNTS   (_____)

Score   Percentage   %

A B C D E F G H I J K L M N O P Q R S T U V W X Y Z

Verbal Reasoning Test 29

1) The same two letters in the same order will complete all six words below. Write these letters inside the brackets.

   p___s   f___e   s___rry   p___mp   c___b   g___tton   (_____)

2) Underline the word which is most similar in meaning to the word in capitals.

   BUCCANEER: sailor   pirate   captain   frigate   soldier

3) Notice how the second word of each pair has been formed from the first, then write the missing word.

   burden, bun   taper, tar   treaty, _____

4) Underline the word which would come in the middle if the words below were arranged to form a sentence.

   Sir Everest climbed Edmund Hilary 1953 In May Mount

5) In a certain code **HMBDMCHZQX** means **INCENDIARY**. What would **EHQDRSNQL** mean in the same code? (_____)

6) Write the word which has both these meanings.
   (a) a number of things in a straight line
   (b) a fierce quarrel   (_____)

7) Complete this analogy: **Singer** is to **music** as **actor** is to _____

8) In the sentence below, four consecutive letters spell the name of a part of the human anatomy. Write this word inside the brackets.

   You should not pack needless things in your holiday luggage.   (_____)

9) Inside the brackets write the same letter which will end the first word and begin the second word of each pair.

   TIN (___) URT   **TO (___) AM**   **BA (___) EARN**

10) Robin is heavier than Rachael but weighs less than Simon. Who is the heaviest?
                                                                                 (_____)

11) Underline the word which describes a person who is old and weak.

    emaciated   ancient   decrepit   sluggish   poorly   ill

A B C D E F G H I J K L M N O P Q R S T U V W X Y Z

12) The second word below is made by rearranging the letters of the first word. Rearrange the letters of the third word in the same way to find the missing word.

   LEPER : REPEL :: REWARD : _____

13) Which letter of the word **PREDICTABLITY** is closest to the middle of the alphabet?   (____)

14) These two rows of squares represent two words. The letters in the lower squares are the same as those directly above them. Study the clues, then write the words.

   ☐☐☐☐☐☐   a ghost or spectre
   ☐ ☐☐☐   to take short fast shallow breaths

15) Underline the word which is the odd one out.

   meadow   paddock   grassland   pasture   field   park

16) Inside the brackets write the word which rhymes with the word in capitals and corresponds to the meaning given.

   SLUICE: a loop in a rope used by a hangman   (_____)

17) One word from the five on the left can be joined to one word from the five on the right to form a compound word. Underline the two words.

   (food, water, juice, drink, swallow)   (house, garage, church, shed, temple)

18) The four words on the left are alike in some way. One word on the right also has this likeness. Underline this word.

   (dine, file, give, pike)   (gave, milk, pier, rise)

19) Inside the brackets, write the seven-letter word needed to complete the unfinished word.

   A _____ buss is a 17th century firearm.   (_____)

20) Underline the two words inside the brackets which go best with the two words in capitals.

   CHURCH : ALTAR   (sing, pew, store, signs, crucifix, booklet)

A B C D E F G H I J K L M N O P Q R S T U V W X Y Z

Verbal Reasoning Test 30

1) Underline the two words below which are most similar in meaning.

   high   precocious   slow   tight   immature   premature

2) Below is a line from a crossword puzzle together with its clue. Complete the word by writing one letter only in each blank square.

   | C | | N | | | | C | | to assemble or put something together

3) Insert the missing word which continues this word pattern.

   flew, flue   blew, blue   dew, _____

4) Move one letter from the first word and place it into the second word to make two new words. Write the two new words in the spaces provided.

   BLUSH and **PEAS** = _____ and _____

5) If the code for **PUSH** is **OSPD**, what is the code for **SHOVE**?
   (_____)

6) Underline the word which is the group name for each of the others.

   marmoset   capuchin   tamarin   primate   macaque   lemur

7) Underline the two words inside the brackets which go best with the two words in capitals.

   HELMET : CROWN   (scarf, bowler, earrings, gloves, stetson)

8) Inside the brackets write the letter which will end the first word and begin the second.
   WAN (___) EMON

9) The same four letters occur in all five words below. Make three different four-letter words from them.

   PARTNERS   TEASPOON   PARENTS   PERSONA   ENTRAP
   (_____ and _____ and _____)

10) If arranged alphabetically, what positions in the alphabet do the vowels in the word **RESIDUAL** occupy?   (_____)

11) Complete this analogy: **Dog** is to **snout** as **bird** is to _____

60   © 2012 Stephen Curran

A B C D E F G H I J K L M N O P Q R S T U V W X Y Z

12) Underline the word which can be made from some or all of the letters of the word **ESTABLISHMENT**, using each letter not more than once.

   HARMLESS   UNICORN   SHAMELESS   MEANEST   RUINED

13) Write the next two terms in this letter series.

   TBV   UDU   VFT   WHS   _____   _____

14) The same two letters in the same order will complete all six words below. Write these letters inside the brackets.

   ro___s   n___ice   l___s   fl___sam   j___ter   bl___ch (_____)

15) Complete the sentence below by writing the same word in both spaces.

   Every _____ detail of the task had to be completed in one _____ .

16) Inside the brackets write the word which rhymes with the word in capitals and corresponds to the meaning given.

   DAYS: to move something to a higher position   (_____)

17) Underline the word which would come in the middle if the words below were arranged to form a sentence.

   bread loaves of thirteen equates A dozen to baker's

18) The four words on the left are alike in some way. One word on the right also has this likeness. Underline this word.

   (drift, brass, cliff, print)   (queue, steel, wrath, niece)

19) Inside the brackets write two letters which will end the first word and begin the second.
   DEA (_____) WART

20) Underline the word which does not fit in with the others.

   cabbage   onion   lettuce   brocolli   avocado   radish

Score [ ]   Percentage [ ]%

A B C D E F G H I J K L M N O P Q R S T U V W X Y Z

Verbal Reasoning Test 31

1) Make a word from the letters which remain after the word **SPLAYS** has been made from the letters of the three words **SILLY**, **SAP** and **TEE**. (_____)

2) Underline the two words inside the brackets which go best with the two words in capitals.

   HOSPITAL : WARD   (clinic, patient, injection, theatre, nurse)

3) Rearrange the capital letters below to form a word corresponding to the meaning given.

   SPOTOCU: a sea creature with eight limbs   (_____)

4) Complete this analogy by underlining one word from each set of brackets.

   Rugby is to (penalty, ball, referee, corner) as **cricket** is to (net, set, serve, umpire)

5) If **HYENA** in code is **FACPY**, then the code **HCAMYN** would mean which word? (_____)

6) Observe how the word inside the brackets has been formed in the example given, then write the missing word.

   CHORE (CABAL) ABYSMAL   PULSE (_____) MIXTURE

7) These two rows of squares represent two words. The letters in the first row of squares are the same as those directly below them. Study the clues, then write the words.

   P _ R _ _ _   a root vegetable
   _ _ _ P   to cut or slice

8) One word from the five on the left can be joined to one word from the five on the right to form a compound word. Underline the two words.

   (dog, fox, cat, cow, donkey)   (hat, coat, shoe, glove, vest)

9) Paul's father's brother, John, is 7 years older than his sibling. Paul was born when John was 30. Paul is now 19 years old. How old is his father? (_____)

10) Underline the word which is the group name for each of the others.

    comedian   actor   magician   artiste   juggler   clown

A B C D E F G H I J K L M N O P Q R S T U V W X Y Z

11) Write the next two terms in this letter series.

    BGR   **DIP**   **FKN**   **HML**   _____   _____

12) Underline the word which does not fit in with the others.

    emblem   symbol   tattoo   brand   mark   scratch

13) Below is a line from a crossword puzzle together with its clue. Complete the word by writing one letter only in each blank square.

    ☐ ☐ N ☐ ☐ L   to hide

14) Move one letter from the first word and place it into the second word to make two new words. Write the two new words in the spaces provided.

    GRATE and **WEST** = _____ and _____

15) Underline the word which cannot be made from some or all of the letters of the word **CONSEQUENTIAL**, using each letter not more than once.

    CLEANEST   ANTIQUES   TENSION   SEQUINS   INCENSE

16) Underline the two words below which are most similar in meaning.

    mute   sombre   cheerful   dissident   speechless   hungry

17) Inside the brackets write the three-letter word which will complete all five words.

    jig___   see___   fore___   fret___   hand___   (_____)

18) In the sentence below, five consecutive letters spell a word meaning the edge of the land. Write this word inside the brackets.

    In winter a drink of hot cocoa still goes down well at bedtime. (_____)

19) In this question there are three pairs of words. Complete the third pair in the same way as the first two pairs. Write the new word inside the brackets.

    (allege, gel)   (active, vet)   (embryo, ____)   (_____)

20) The four words on the left are alike in some way. One word on the right also has this likeness. Underline this word.

    (autumn, biscuit, wrapper, foreign)   (sword, arm, crew, buzzard)

Score ☐ Percentage ☐ %

A B C D E F G H I J K L M N O P Q R S T U V W X Y Z

Verbal Reasoning Test 32

1) Underline the word which cannot be made from some or all of the letters of the word **CAPRICIOUSLY**, using each letter not more than once.

   CRUCIAL   OILY   ACRYLIC   SLURPS   PIOUS

2) Complete this analogy: **Earth** is to **fox** as **warren** is to _____

3) Inside the brackets write two letters which will end the first word and begin the second.
   DET (_____) **ROR**

4) If **HATED** in code is **74532**, then _____ means **DEATH** in the same code.

5) Write the letter which comes between the 4th and 5th vowels in the alphabet and which does not occur in the word **REQUEST**.   (_____)

6) Insert the word which will complete the sentence and rhymes with the word in capital letters.

   SHOOT: Oliver slid down the _____ into the water.

7) Arrange these words in alphabetical order by numbering them 1-5:

   crack (__)   cartel (__)   cautious (__)   cattle (__)   cramped (__)

8) Below is a line from a crossword puzzle together with its clue. Complete the word by writing one letter only in each blank square.

   C □ A □ R □ H □   a terrible disaster

9) Underline the word which describes a person who is not generous in giving or spending money.

   stingy   rude   wealthy   sullen   objectionable   careful

10) In the space provided, write the missing word formed by rearranging the letters of the word in heavy type.

    The BBC asked television **viewers** to complete _____ of various programmes.

11) If **CATTLE** in code is **ZDQWIH**, what does **CDOPBU** represent in the same code?   (_____)

64   © 2012 Stephen Curran

A B C D E F G H I J K L M N O P Q R S T U V W X Y Z

12) Write the word which has both these meanings.
    (a) to become or make something different
    (b) coins of small denomination   (_____)

13) Observe how the word inside the brackets has been formed in the example given, then write the missing word.

    DESPAIR (FARES) FROST   SCHOOLS (_____) PUPIL

14) Using all the letters of the word **SCHOLARS** only once, two other words were made. If one of the words was **CAR**, what was the other word?   (_____)

15) One word from the five on the left can be joined to one word from the five on the right to form a compound word. Underline the two words.

    (oil, wood, fish, dash, walk)   (away, sea, tray, board, light)

16) Underline the two words inside the brackets which go best with the two words in capitals.

    PEAK : HILL   (mountain, cliff, platform, ridge, roof, hillock)

17) Rearrange the capital letters below to form a word which completes the sentence.

    SEERNU: Before mooring the boat he checked the ropes were tied securely to _____ it would not be swept away.

18) The same four letters occur in all six words below. Make two different words from them.

    TERSELY   STABLE   TRANSLATE   STENCIL   RESULT   BLEATS
                                       (_____ and _____)

19) Three of the four words below are given in code. The codes are not written in the same order as the words and one code is missing.

    BALE   LATE   STEM   FITS   3478   1943   6257
    a) Find the code for **TABLES**.   (_____)
    b) Find the word for **178257**.   (_____)

20) Two letters in the alphabet, separated by one other, form a word when spelt backwards. Write this word.   (_____)

Score [ ]   Percentage [ ] %

A B C D E F G H I J K L M N O P Q R S T U V W X Y Z

Verbal Reasoning Test 33

1) Underline the word which cannot be made from some or all of the letters of the word **CIVILISATION**, using each letter not more than once.

   SILICON   ICONIC   ITALICS   VIOLINS   COILS

2) These two rows of squares represent two words. The letters in the first row of squares are the same as those directly below them. Study the clues, then write the words.

   ☐ ☐☐   a portable container or box
   ☐☐☐☐☐☐☐   to diminish in size, strength or amount

3) Underline two words, one from each set of brackets, which are opposite in meaning.

   (decaying, sweet, bitter, harsh, sublime)   (pickle, dry, meaty, fresh, caustic)

4) Write the next two terms in this letter series.

   WFW   YIA   ALE   COI   _____   _____

5) Underline the word which is the group name for each of the others.

   chameleon   lizard   iguana   gecko   skink   monitor

6) If all the letters of the word **SCANTILY** were removed from the alphabet, which would be the tenth letter in the new alphabet?   (___)

7) One word from the five on the left can be joined to one word from the five on the right to form a compound word. Underline the two words.

   (see, speak, hear, feel, smell)   (five, number, ten, two, add)

8) Inside the brackets write the four-letter word which will complete all five words.

   ___chat   ___fire   ___fill   ___cloth   ___log   (_____)

9) In the sentence below, six consecutive letters spell the name of a look-out or guard. Write this word inside the brackets.

   The supermarket incorrectly sent rye bread in the delivery.   (_____)

10) Underline the word which does not fit in with the others.

    crochet   quaver   stave   minim   semi-breve   rest

66   © 2012 Stephen Curran

A B C D E F G H I J K L M N O P Q R S T U V W X Y Z

11) Carol, Jasmeen, Pryanka, Sandra and Sophia all ran a cross-country race. Sandra finished four places ahead of Pryanka who was behind Jasmeen. Carol finished just ahead of Sandra but three places ahead of Sophia. Who finished last out of all the runners? (_____)

12) In this question there are three pairs of words. Complete the third pair in the same way as the first two pairs. Write the new word inside the brackets.

   (lancet, late)   (tinged, tide)   (bolden, _____)   (_____)

13) In the space provided, write the missing word formed by rearranging the letters of the word in heavy type.

   It was a thin sheet of **crimson** paper only 120 _____ thick.

14) Move one letter from the first word and place it into the second word to make two new words. Write the two new words in the spaces provided.

   CHAFE and **TERM** = _____ and _____

15) Rearrange the letters of the word in capitals to form a word corresponding to the meaning given.

   COILED: quiet and easy to control   (_____)

16) Observe how the word inside the brackets has been formed in the example given, then write the missing word.

   CONDOR (FROWN) SWIFT   HIDDEN (_____) LANKY

17) Underline the word which is similar in meaning to the word in capitals.

   RUMINATE: drink   ponder   wander   climb   cuddle

18) The second word below is formed by rearranging the letters of the first word. Rearrange the letters of the third word in the same way to find the missing word.

   PEALS : LAPSE :: REAPS : _____

19) Make a word from the letters which remain after the word **CAUTIONARY** has been made from the letters of the three words **AURORA**, **LITANY** and **COY**. (_____)

20) Below is a line from a crossword puzzle together with its clue. Complete the word by writing one letter only in each blank square.

   D ☐ ☐ R ☐ T   to take something away

   Score ☐   Percentage ☐ %

A B C D E F G H I J K L M N O P Q R S T U V W X Y Z

Verbal Reasoning Test 34

1) The same five letters occur in all five words below. Make a word from them.

   CREMATION   SANCTIONER   ROMANTI   CERATINS   TRANSIT

   (_____)

2) Below is a line from a crossword puzzle together with its clue. Complete the word by writing one letter only in each blank square.

   ☐ L ☐ ☐ I ☐ ☐ R   a Roman slave who fought for entertainment.

3) Write the next two terms in this letter series.

   CT   EQ   HO   LL   QJ   ____   ____

4) Inside the brackets write two letters which will end the first word and begin the second.

   SMI (____) ASH

5) Complete this analogy by underlining one word from each set of brackets.

   Lance is to (weapon, pole, fight, joust) as **sword** is to (sharp, fence, kill, thrust)

6) Underline the word which would come last if these words were arranged in alphabetical order.

   fragile   frugal   friendship   frigate   frequent

7) Form a word from the letters which are contained in the first half of the alphabet in the word **STUPIDLY**.   (_____)

8) These two rows of squares represent two words. The letters in the first row of squares are the same as those directly below them. Study the clues, then write the words.

   ☐☐ ☐☐   great in size or importance
   ☐☐☐☐☐   a compelling desire for food

9) If **WINTER** in code is **QNJWCS**, what does **UZPXKO** stand for in the same code?   (_____)

10) In the sentence below, five consecutive letters spell the name of a token pinned on clothing to show membership. Write this word inside the brackets.

    Sindbad gets marooned after he sets sail from Basra.   (_____)

A B C D E F G H I J K L M N O P Q R S T U V W X Y Z

11) Rearrange the last four letters of the word **EARLIEST** in two different ways so they form two different words. (_____ and _____)

12) In the space provided, write the missing word formed by rearranging the letters of the word in heavy type.

    The joiner used his **plane** to smooth a _____ of wood.

13) Underline two words, one from each set of brackets, which are most similar in meaning.

    (cajole, move, compel, carry)   (hurry, coax, shout, cry)

14) The four words on the left are alike in some way. One word on the right also has this likeness. Underline this word.

    (cheer, shudder, stretch, bequeath)   (geese, peach, cenotaph, track)

15) Insert the word which will complete the sentence and rhymes with the word in capital letters.

    MEET: They bought a three-piece _____ from the furniture store.

16) In this question there are three pairs of words. Complete the third pair in the same way as the first two pairs. Write the new word in the space provided.

    (weekend, weed)   (grapple, gape)   (braille, ____)   (_____)

17) Underline the word which cannot be made from some or all of the letters of the word **CONGREGATION**, using each letter not more than once.

    IGNORE   CANTER   ONGOING   REACTION   CREATE

18) Three of the four words below are given in code. The codes are not written in the same order as the words and one code is missing.

    STAY   REST   BACK   TEAR   5374   8216   7429

    a) Find the code for **YEAST**.   (_____)
    b) Find the word for **85247**.   (_____)

19) In the space provided, write the missing word formed by rearranging the letters of the word in heavy type.

    You can **expect** to get the right answer on a calculator _____ when you key in the wrong numbers.

20) Underline the word which does not fit in with the others.

    wind   fire   earth   water   sand

A B C D E F G H I J K L M N O P Q R S T U V W X Y Z

Verbal Reasoning Test 35

1) Underline the word which does not fit in with the others.

   gale   tempest   hurricane   tornado   tsunami   cyclone

2) Rearrange the letters of the word in capitals to form a word corresponding to the meaning given.

   DETAIL: the pupils become wider or larger   (_____)

3) If **73142** means **DOZEN**, what does **13247** mean in the same code?   (_____)

4) Below is a line from a crossword puzzle together with its clue. Complete the word by writing one letter only in each blank square.

   ☐ A ☐ ☐ L R ☐   armed horsemen

5) Underline the two words below which are similar in meaning.

   questionable   sensible   susceptible   indifferent   vulnerable

6) In this question there are three pairs of words. Complete the third pair in the same way as the first two pairs. Write the new word in the space provided.

   (rapid, raid)   (metal, meal)   (dance, ____)   (_____)

7) Write the next two terms in this letter series.

   GBC   IEG   KHK   MKO   ____   ____

8) If **SHARE** in code is **UKCUG**, what does **TDVLQK** stand for in the same code?   (_____)

9) Inside the brackets write the same letter which will end the first word and begin the second word of each pair.

   FLA (___) ART   BLO (___) IN   CHO (___) ANT

10) Make a word from the letters which remain after the words **SIR** and **TRENDS** have been made from the letters of the word **DARSTARDLINESS**.   (_____)

70   © 2012 Stephen Curran

A B C D E F G H I J K L M N O P Q R S T U V W X Y Z

11) Three of the four words below are given in code. The codes are not written in the same order as the words and one code is missing.

    VEST   DIRE   RATE   SEAT   4392   5683   8923

a) Find the code for **STRIDE**. (_____)

b) Find the word for **23943**. (_____)

12) In the sentence below, five consecutive letters spell the name of a large mammal. Write this word inside the brackets.

The sampan darted across the river propelled by its oarsmen. (_____)

13) One word from the four on the left can be joined to one word from the four on the right to form a compound word. Underline the two words.

(stop, fire, cook, pan, oven)   (go, shoot, play, storm, burn)

14) In the sentence below, the word in capital letters has had three consecutive letters taken out. These three letters will make one correctly spelt word without changing their order. Write this word inside the brackets.

In the winter months Stephen ate a large bowl of PORGE every day. (_____)

15) Inside the brackets write the three-letter word which will complete all five words.

___ash   ___belly   ___luck   ___hole   ___shot   (_____)

16) Underline two words, one from each set of brackets, which are opposite in meaning.

(content, obese, righteous, rabid)   (immoral, oblivious, tearful, fearful)

17) The same two letters in the same order will complete all six words below. Write these letters inside the brackets.

l___y   k___l   f___m   j___t   qu___t   dr___l   (_____)

18) These two rows of squares represent two words. The letters in the first row of squares are the same as those directly below them. Study the clues, then write the words.

☐☐☐ to show concern

☐☐☐☐☐ stroke affectionately

19) Observe how the word inside the brackets has been formed in the example given, then write the missing word.

CRANE (RANGE) ANGEL   STOUR (_____) SWEET

20) Which letter in the word **SANCTUARY** comes nearest to the thirteenth consonant in the alphabet? (___)

Score ☐ Percentage ☐ %

A B C D E F G H I J K L M N O P Q R S T U V W X Y Z

Verbal Reasoning Test 36

1) Underline the word which is the odd one out.

   butter   mustard   yoghurt   milk   cheese   curd

2) In this question there are three pairs of words. Complete the third pair in the same way as the first two pairs. Write the new word in the space provided.

   (stripe, pier)   (consent, nets)   (desist, _____)   (_____)

3) Write the next two terms in this letter series.

   DX   **CC**   **AG**   **XJ**   _____   _____

4) Three of the four words below are given in code. The codes are not written in the same order as the words and one code is missing.

   BALL   TRIP   PART   BETS   **4593   1248   1766**

   a) Find the code for **STRAP**.   (_____)
   b) Find the word for **16284**.   (_____)

5) Move one letter from the first word and place it into the second word to make two new words. Write the two new words in the spaces provided.

   CLEMENT and **COMPETE** = _____ and _____

6) Complete this analogy by underlining one word from each set of brackets.

   Sheath is to (shield, spear, belt, knife) as **silo** is to (earth, hay, grain, liquid)

7) In the sentence below, the word in capital letters has had three consecutive letters taken out. These three letters will make one correctly spelt word without changing their order. Write this word inside the brackets.

   The doctor's PANTS waited for his surgery to begin.   (_____)

8) Observe how the word inside the brackets has been formed in the example given, then write the missing word.

   POTATO (TOTE) LEEK   RIPPLE (_____) MELT

9) In the space provided, write the missing word formed by rearranging the letters of the word in heavy type.

   The farmer's **German** shepherd dog was eating food from the animals' _____ .

10) One word from the four on the left can be joined to one word from the four on the right to form a compound word. Underline the two words.

    (minute, hour, second, time)   (segment, piece, half, slice)

A B C D E F G H I J K L M N O P Q R S T U V W X Y Z

11) If **LAUNCH** in code is **OZTMXS**, what does **ILXPVG** stand for in the same code? (_____)

12) In the sentence below, seven consecutive letters spell an adjective meaning 'having no doubts'. Write this word inside the brackets.

   The garlic and onions processed through the mincer tainted everything else.
   (_____)

13) The four words on the left are alike in some way. One word on the right also has this likeness. Underline this word.

   (mapping, dossier, potter, terror)   (tempt, scotch, stretch, sadden)

14) Below is a line from a crossword puzzle together with its clue. Complete the word by writing one letter only in each blank square.

   ☐ ☐ R N ☐ ☐ E the widespread slaughter of people

15) Underline the two words inside the brackets which go best with the two words in capitals.

   PIKE : BREAM   (frog, roach, newt, vole, salmon)

16) Underline the word which is opposite in meaning to the word in capitals.

   CHIDE: praise   reproach   harass   nag   compliment

17) Below are two pairs of words. One word from the list will go equally well with both pairs of words in the brackets. Underline this word.
   FEARLESS   CLEVER   LOUD   ROBUST   WEAK
   (STRONG, HEALTHY)   (DERTERMINED, FORCEFUL)

18) These two rows of squares represent two words. The letters in the first row of squares are the same as those directly below them. Study the clues, then write the words.

   ☐☐☐☐☐   it can be eaten
   ☐☐☐☐☐☐ easy to believe

19) Underline the word which cannot be made from some or all of the letters of the word **CONTEMPLATE** using each letter not more than once.

   PLANET   CAPON   CATTLEMAN   TENTACLE   MOTTLE

20) Using all the letters of the word **INEVITABLE** only once, three other words were made. If two of the words were **EVE** and **BIN**, what was the other word? (_____)

Score ☐   Percentage ☐ %

A B C D E F G H I J K L M N O P Q R S T U V W X Y Z

Verbal Reasoning Test 37

1) Underline the word below which can be made from some or all of the letters of the word **INSINUATED**, using each letter not more than once.

    STRAINED   INITIALS   SAINTS   UNSEATED   STAINED   DAUNTED

2) Write in alphabetical order the five letters in the word **IMPORTANTLY** which are consecutive in the alphabet.   (_____)

3) These two rows of squares represent two words. The letters in the first row of squares are the same as those directly below them. Study the clues, then write the words.

    ☐ ☐ ☐   to sink down in the middle
    ☐ ☐ ☐ ☐ ☐   informal language expressions

4) Observe how the word inside the brackets has been formed in the example given, then write the missing word.

    OUTPUT (PROP) SPRY   SENTRY(_____) SCAM

5) Jack arrived at school earlier than Simon who was ahead of Edward but later than Ben. George arrived behind Ben but before Jack. Who arrived first? (_____)

6) In the space provided, write the missing word formed by rearranging the letters of the word in heavy type.

    Food allergies are a **pointer** to an intolerance of a specific _____ .

7) One word from the four on the left can be joined to one word from the four on the right to form a compound word. Underline the two words.

    (travel, space, alien, star)   (drink, ate, back, bite)

8) The same two letters in the same order will complete all six words below. Write these letters inside the brackets.

    h___r   r___n   v___l   b___ng   d___ty   b___ge   (_____)

9) In this question there are three pairs of words. Complete the third pair in the same way as the first two pairs. Write the new word in the space provided.

    (dissent, net)   (noblest, set)   (unsure, ____)   (_____)

10) Rearrange the letters of the word in capitals to form a word corresponding to the meaning given.

    ASSUAGE: a casing stuffed with meat and other ingredients
                                                        (_____)

74   © 2012 Stephen Curran

A B C D E F G H I J K L M N O P Q R S T U V W X Y Z

11) Underline the two words which do not fit in with the others.

   brakes   service   engine   gearbox   repair   tyres

12) Underline the two words, one from each set of brackets, which are most similar in meaning.

   (collate, collude, collide, collect)   (conscript, conquer, conceal, conspire)

13) Insert the missing word which continues this word pattern.

   room, real   doom, deal   zoom, _____

14) Make two words from the letters which remain after the word **EMANCIPATES** has been made from the letters of the two words **COMBINE** and **SEPARATE**.   (_____ and _____)

15) Underline the word which is similar in meaning to the word in capitals.

   ACQUIRE: proclaim   procure   prospect   profess   prosecute

16) Underline the word which does not fit in with the others.

   beagle   terrier   tabby   collie   boxer   poodle

17) In the sentence below, the word in capital letters has had three consecutive letters taken out. These three letters will make one correctly spelt word without changing their order. Write this word inside the brackets.

   Emily **PRISED** playing her flute for one hour each day.   (_____)

18) If **BANDIT** in code is **DXPAKQ**, what does **QRVICT** stand for in the same code?   (_____)

19) In the sentence below, six consecutive letters spell the name of a gardening tool. Write this word inside the brackets.

   The new bistro welcomed its first customers and rewarded them with a complimentary bottle of wine.   (_____)

20) Inside the brackets write the same letter which will end the first word and begin the second word of each pair.

   PILO (___) AINT   OCCUL (___) RAVERSE

A B C D E F G H I J K L M N O P Q R S T U V W X Y Z

Verbal Reasoning Test 38

1) Below is a line from a crossword puzzle together with its clue. Complete the word by writing one letter only in each blank square.

   ☐ P ☐ H ☐   a lack of interest or energy

2) The four words on the left are alike in some way. One word on the right also has this likeness. Underline this word.

   (tough, churn, thunder, hearing)   (noise, weak, larger, pathetic)

3) If **LIQUID** in code is **RNUXKE**, what does **LQYLFT** stand for in the same code?   (_____)

4) Underline the word which is the odd one out.

   iron   carbon   oil   oxygen   zinc   silver

5) Write the next two terms in this letter series.

   MRY   OTS   RVN   VXJ   _____   _____

6) Below are two pairs of words. One word from the list will go equally well with both pairs of words in the brackets. Underline this word.

   DUST   SCOUR   WASH   POLISH   STALK

   (HUNT, SEARCH)   (CLEAN, SCRUB)

7) Complete this sentence by inserting the word with the opposite meaning to the word in heavy type.

   They sought shelter by moving from **sparse** wasteland into _____ forest.

8) Inside the brackets write the word which rhymes with the word in capitals and corresponds to the meaning given.

   ROUGH: to mislead someone by presenting a confident front   (_____)

9) Underline the word which describes a person with a playful, joking disposition.

   rumbustious   jocular   stoical   generous   laborious

10) Inside the brackets write the same letter which will end the first word and begin the second word of each pair.

    DIVE (___) EAD   SAVE (___) OVE   SOU (___) ENT

A B C D E F G H I J K L M N O P Q R S T U V W X Y Z

11) These two rows of squares represent two words. The letters in the first row of squares are the same as those directly below them. Study the clues, then write the words.

   ☐☐☐☐☐   a stand for an artist's canvas
   ☐☐☐☐☐   a small carnivore with a slender body

12) How many letters in the word **PUNCTILIOUS** come in the first half of the alphabet? (_____)

13) Complete this analogy by underlining one word from each set of brackets.

    Cobra is to (snarl, strike, kill, fangs) as **skunk** is to (smell, bite, stink, spray)

14) One word from the five on the left can be joined to one word from the five on the right to form a compound word. Underline the two words.

    (single, fish, river, float, soft)   (sink, water, pillow, sea, bed)

15) Underline the word which would come fourth if these words were arranged in alphabetical order.

    truncheon   trusting   truculent   truffle   truthful

16) Underline the word which is the group name for each of the others.

    plate   cup   saucer   platter   tableware   tureen

17) Observe how the word inside the brackets has been formed in the example given, then write the missing word.

    SWEAT (STARE) ALERT   PETAL (_____) TEETH

18) In the sentence below, five consecutive letters describe a latin American dance. Write this word inside the brackets.

    A good business will attempt to maintain universal satisfaction among its customers. (_____)

19) In the space provided, write the missing word formed by rearranging the letters of the word in heavy type.

    One Olympic **relay** team was disqualified when they left their mark too _____.

20) Move one letter from the first word and place it into the second word to make two new words. Write the two new words in the spaces provided.

    BOUND and **DEBT** = _____ and _____

Score ☐ Percentage ☐%

© 2012 Stephen Curran

A B C D E F G H I J K L M N O P Q R S T U V W X Y Z

Verbal Reasoning Test 39

1) These two rows of squares represent two words. The letters in the lower squares are the same as those directly above them. Study the clues, then write the words.

   ☐☐☐☐☐☐☐   exact and accurate
   ☐☐   ☐☐☐   to lever open

2) In the space provided, write the missing word formed by rearranging the letters of the word in heavy type.

   The **leader** of the gang was also a drug _____ .

3) Notice how the second word of each pair has been formed from the first, then write the missing word.

   lenient, lent   reprise, rise   cashew, _____

4) In the sentence below, seven consecutive letters spell the name of a sport. Write this word inside the brackets.

   After the hailstorm, a beautiful rainbow lingered in the sky for nearly an hour.   (_____)

5) Write the next two terms in this letter series.

   FG   CI   ZK   WM _____ _____

6) Underline the word which does not fit in with the others.

   Niger   Amazon   Windermere   Euphrates   Severn   Nile

7) Underline the two words below which are most opposite in meaning.

   count   break   polish   neglect   treasure   display

8) Move one letter from the first word and place it into the second word to make two new words. Write the two new words in the spaces provided.

   STEWING and **ANGLED** = _____ and _____

9) One word from the five on the left can be joined to one word from the five on the right to form a compound word. Underline the two words.

   (jam, butter, syrup, spread, honey)   (brush, broom, comb, rake, ribbon)

10) If **TEASE** in code is **GVZHV**, what does **ZMMLB** stand for in the same code?   (_____)

A B C D E F G H I J K L M N O P Q R S T U V W X Y Z

11) The same two letters in the same order will complete all six words below. Write these letters inside the brackets.

    m___e   d___k   w___y   g___d   a___s   tw___l   (_____)

12) Complete the sentence by underlining the correct answer.
Compared with an 8 metre square, a 2 metre square is _____ as small in area.

TWICE   FOUR TIMES   SIXTEEN TIMES   HALF

13) Write down the second to the fifth and the ninth to the twelfth letters of the sentence you are now reading and rearrange them to make another number. Write this word inside the brackets.   (_____)

14) Complete this analogy by underlining one word from each set of brackets.

Mad is to (nasty, crazy, silly) as **sensible** is to (stupid, sane, mature)

15) In the sentence below, the word in capital letters has had three consecutive letters taken out. These three letters will make one correctly spelt word without changing their order. Write this word inside the brackets.

The **ORING** satellite beamed transmissions to Earth.   (_____)

16) Underline the two words inside the brackets which go best with the two words in capitals.

SUGAR : SYRUP   (jelly, cake, molasses, dessert, honey)

17) Using all the letters of the word **NUMERATOR** only once, two other words were made. If one of the words was **TUNER**, what was the other word? (_____)

18) Underline the word below which can be made from some or all of the letters of the word **PERSPIRATION**, using each letter not more than once.

    EARNEST   PISTONS   TERRAPIN   APPRAISE   RESIST

19) Write the word which has both these meanings.
    (a) to create television programmes
    (b) fruits or vegetables grown on a farm   (_____)

20) Underline the word which describes behaviour which is unpredictable.

    evasive   erratic   erroneous   eccentric   eclectic

Score   Percentage   %

© 2012 Stephen Curran

A B C D E F G H I J K L M N O P Q R S T U V W X Y Z

Verbal Reasoning Test 40

1) Rearrange the letters of the word in capitals to form a word corresponding to the meaning given.

   THICH: to temporarily fasten a rope   (_____)

2) Underline the word which does not fit in with the others.

   swim   walk   bathe   bravely   think   listen   shout

3) Insert the missing word which continues this word pattern.

   quick, lick   quake, lake   quash, _____

4) One word from the five on the left can be joined to one word from the five on the right to form a compound word. Underline the two words.

   (lose, hard, down, quick, blue)   (lead, sand, legs, road, door)

5) Underline the word which would come last if these words were arranged in alphabetical order.

   remember   reminder   remonstrate   remittance   remain

6) Inside the brackets write two letters which will end the first word and begin the second.

   CALIB (_____) **TURN**

7) Underline the word which describes a vegetable of the gourd family.

   squid   grape   squash   quince   squelch

8) Move one letter from the first word and place it into the second word to make two new words. Write the two new words in the spaces provided.

   CHEAT and **STEP** = _____ and _____

9) Underline the word which would come fifth if the words below were arranged to form a sentence.

   see of impossible a glass pane is to opaque through It

10) If **BOULES** in code is **DNWKGR**, what is the word for **EQQPWDV** in the same code?   (_____)

11) Write the next two terms in this letter series.

    WXY   **YYB**   **BAD**   **DDG**   **GHI**   _____ _____

ABCDEFGHIJKLMNOPQRSTUVWXYZ

12) Below is a line from a crossword puzzle together with its clue. Complete the word by writing one letter only in each blank square.

☐ R ☐ C I ☐ ☐   a copy of a drawing, map, or plan

13) The words for three of the four codes are given below. The words are not written in the same order as the codes and one word is missing.

2457   5823   1946   7423   NAIL   MIST   TIME

a) Find the word for **579231**.   (_____)

b) Find the code for **ALIEN**.   (_____)

14) In the space provided, write the missing word formed by rearranging the letters of the word in heavy type.

Acres of ground had to be cleared to build the Olympic Stadium to enable athletic _____ and field events to take place.

15) Below are two pairs of words. One word from the list will go equally well with both pairs of words in the brackets. Underline this word.

GOLD   PUSH   SOUND   RING   PROFESSIONAL

(BELL, ECHO)   (JEWELLERY, BOXING)

16) Complete this analogy by underlining one word from each set of brackets.

Cello is to (zither, banjo, violin, harpsichord) as **bassoon** is to (trombone, trumpet, tuba, oboe)

17) Rearrange the middle five letters of the word **RESOURCES** so they form a word.   (_____)

18) Underline the word which cannot be made from some or all of the letters of the word **HAILSTONES**, using each letter not more than once.

LOATHES   SALIENT   HEATH   TALONS   SEASON

19) Write the word which has both these meanings.
(a) a publication issued at regular intervals
(b) a container that holds bullets in a gun   (_____)

20) Inside the brackets write the four-letter word needed to complete the unfinished word.

To be absor _____ is to be capable of soaking up liquid. (_____)

Score ☐   Percentage ☐ %

Notes

Answers

*11+ Verbal Reasoning
Year 5-7 GL & Other
Styles Testbook 2*

Test 1
1) straw
2) ARMED
3) i
4) S, W
5) CAR or ARC
6) seven
7) FAT
8) clamber
9) o
10) hide
11) dust
12) brush
13) EAST
14) TRAY
15) BATS
16) port
17) CHEAT
18) weight
19) mean & generous
20) keen

Test 2
1) s
2) crowd
3) roved
4) TIP or PIT
5) T
6) VBCMQOQO
7) hay
8) drift & glide
9) stubble
10) transmits & orbits
11) under
12) SOUTH
13) 4531423
14) J,G
15) ROUND
16) sparrow
17) most
18) mentor
19) metre & fathom
20) uncle

Test 3
1) turn
2) toast
3) WATER
4) liner
5) CHAT
6) MEANER
7) abolish
8) three
9) MN, PK
10) MISSILES
11) brewed
12) bicycle
13) EDIT
14) easy & onerous
15) denounce
16) object
17) PEAT or TAPE
18) STYLES
19) vent
20) showed & stopped

Test 4
1) Yen
2) badger
3) H
4) P
5) over
6) buoy
7) SAT
8) cedar
9) 4, 1, 3, 2, 5
10) rhododendron
11) 96472
12) action
13) VACUUM
14) brevity
15) PET
16) PALE
17) tort
18) enormous
19) SMELL
20) TI, UH

Test 5
1) BDUJWF
2) HP, IQ
3) apple
4) RISK
5) PEDAL
6) rose
7) L
8) GIVING
9) HARE
10) STU
11) send
12) false
13) steel
14) peas
15) put & found
16) elation
17) R
18) address
19) LANCED
20) under

Test 6
1) role
2) TARTS
3) won & drove
4) puny
5) 546325

© 2012 Stephen Curran

11+ Verbal Reasoning Year 5-7 GL & Other Styles Testbook 2

Answers

6) seized
7) slate
8) I, O, U
9) COILED or DOCILE
10) HEARING
11) stone
12) ENTRAPS
13) M
14) REFINES
15) ban
16) WX, BC
17) rap & knock
18) BUG
19) down
20) F

Test 7
1) prize
2) false
3) drafts
4) thrush
5) RICE
6) RST
7) SVWOPW
8) W
9) lemon
10) PAINT
11) awful
12) fiery & hushed
13) SALUTES
14) BRAISED
15) gaudy & dull
16) great
17) UY, ZD
18) WASTE
19) squirt
20) quash

Test 8
1) B, F, H, L, M, N, T
2) fine
3) SPENT
4) recent
5) durable & tough
6) fished & caught
7) steel
8) pad
9) HEAP & CLAMP
10) CN, HS
11) bed
12) defiant
13) YARD
14) 62597
15) brace
16) rest
17) GLOAT
18) PAN & NAP
19) pertain
20) dough

Test 9
1) mall
2) ADVENT
3) thief
4) j
5) B
6) annoy & irritate
7) old & rushing
8) DEBAR
9) respect & contempt
10) conduct
11) SCENE
12) fly
13) trousers
14) points
15) FED
16) POUND
17) hand
18) a, e, i
19) shine
20) E

Test 10
1) lowed & whinnied
2) A, I, O, U
3) up
4) disobedient
5) PREDICTION
6) MELONS
7) SHED
8) tugs
9) gel
10) HMJNQTF
11) CLIENTELE
12) GREY
13) leg
14) VEINS or VINES
15) US
16) oil
17) CRATE
18) tell
19) deceased & alive
20) PUN

Test 11
1) pound
2) HAMMERS
3) misery
4) NUANCE & ORNAMENT
5) captivating

Answers

*11+ Verbal Reasoning
Year 5-7 GL & Other
Styles Testbook 2*

6) chisel
7) FE or PE
8) NOP
9) 3, 1, 5, 2, 4
10) descend & climb
11) WINTER
12) ALTERED
13) arm
14) SE
15) S
16) RAY
17) OR
18) CHAIN
19) doze
20) CDRJ

Test 12
1) reviled
2) BREAM
3) tinsel
4) EMIGRANTS
5) many & popular
6) DERAILMENTS
7) 42831576
8) BQ, ZW
9) dischord & harmony
10) stream
11) NOON
12) extreme
13) swim
14) hire
15) CRISIS
16) hand
17) numb
18) lack
19) present
20) OIL

Test 13
1) in
2) CN, XP
3) licit
4) Volvo
5) oa
6) wound
7) cot & coat
8) PINTS
9) on & to
10) r
11) bull
12) TINGLES
13) new & taller
14) teacher
15) plough
16) medals
17) CREASE & CEASE
18) kind
19) RIVER
20) TILL or LILT

Test 14
1) KE
2) breast
3) three
4) RAIN or IRAN
5) amuse
6) peal
7) 22 9 3 20 15 18
8) to
9) compassionate
10) AL
11) METRES
12) empires
13) LION

14) SEQUINED
15) bankrupt
16) hawk
17) upset
18) trial
19) RECALL
20) NIB or BIN

Test 15
1) Glasgow
2) LIMP
3) or
4) take & remove
5) oven
6) t
7) rent & sergeant
8) bawls
9) STARE
10) shoe
11) DEAR
12) bush & worth
13) ZOCWPE
14) teals
15) drought
16) start
17) NECESSARY
18) ROCK
19) ONEROUS
20) head & dress

Test 16
1) TE
2) EXHIBITOR
3) impression
4) SAUCES
5) TIER
6) queue

© 2012 Stephen Curran

11+ Verbal Reasoning Year 5-7 GL & Other Styles Testbook 2

Answers

7) NIECE
8) radish
9) Tuesday
10) SUNK
11) hummed
12) MXGLFLDO
13) PEOPLE
14) feigned
15) sidle & idle
16) TELL
17) nose & mouth
18) robust & fragile
19) band
20) flour

Test 17
1) REVISION
2) BOVINE
3) November
4) REPLAYS
5) WEST
6) ham & string
7) C, D, L, M, N, R, S, T
8) NS, SR
9) port
10) HAGGLE
11) tail
12) CWPVWBX & XEWPBVX
13) deteriorate
14) stranger
15) mound
16) mislaid & mild
17) blight
18) steamer
19) GLIB
20) bosun

Test 18
1) lack & lustre
2) adder
3) TAILOR
4) beggar
5) picnic
6) CANS & SCAN
7) genial
8) PEN
9) wake
10) TRUE
11) stable
12) 16832947
13) CHUTE
14) bake & brake
15) PENALTY
16) bulk
17) hot & wet
18) itinerant
19) bank
20) LOAF

Test 19
1) ST
2) solution
3) O
4) CORD
5) sure
6) strong
7) CRYPT
8) PRIM, PROM & ROMP
9) back & stage
10) treasurer
11) provide & pride
12) DROP
13) STEW
14) depth & height

15) TREE
16) cunning
17) estate
18) PONY
19) RAY
20) elbow

Test 20
1) minion
2) TRAILER
3) purse
4) STUD & DUST
5) WFBZ & CBRF
6) ADORATION
7) DE
8) PANG & CRANE
9) cut & out
10) G, E
11) CLAW
12) Sally
13) money
14) tough
15) fade & facade
16) alert
17) rainbow & gold
18) TONED
19) PACT
20) close

Test 21
1) TRANCES
2) POSE & FIEND
3) ML, OJ
4) hole
5) TONGUE
6) combine
7) amber

Answers

*11+ Verbal Reasoning
Year 5-7 GL & Other
Styles Testbook 2*

8) INFAMOUS
9) AIDE
10) heave & lug
11) teal
12) S
13) abacus
14) result
15) cart & clarinet
16) CROP
17) grant
18) LAGER
19) FLAILED
20) weight & scales

Test 22
1) RECKON
2) REMAIN
3) cockle & oyster
4) spire
5) DIN
6) others
7) 1, 4, 5, 2, 3
8) pâté
9) BLOW
10) FLY
11) RHYME
12) raucous
13) gnat
14) UNIFORM
15) scars
16) TARNISH
17) action
18) SPHERES
19) BELT
20) toe & cap

Test 23
1) ape
2) task
3) react
4) WEATHER
5) shimmer
6) SCHOLAR
7) penicillin & antibacterial
8) defect
9) in
10) CARE
11) cannon
12) INANE
13) VIOLENT
14) fly & flowery
15) CDE, BCD
16) braid
17) cross & wind
18) POOR
19) QUALIFY
20) AFGBC

Test 24
1) hull & keel
2) FSIEI
3) litre
4) TAUT
5) OR
6) 13, 6, 16, 17, 2, 19, 5
7) harp & harpoon
8) on
9) clothed
10) S
11) drowned
12) morose & cheerful

13) PAYMENT
14) way & fare
15) Mexico
16) dreadful
17) ACTS
18) tile
19) miracle
20) CAUTION

Test 25
1) JZ, KW
2) unlikely
3) CLASPS
4) refuse
5) DEFIANT
6) PINED
7) TEPID
8) car & tyres
9) OZEVVTW
10) dusty
11) occlude & block
12) yr
13) PRODUCT
14) win
15) candle
16) winch
17) MASH
18) TREACLE
19) just & ice
20) dice

Test 26
1) crack
2) profession
3) Friday
4) relates
5) LOGICAL

© 2012 Stephen Curran

11+ Verbal Reasoning Year 5-7 GL & Other Styles Testbook 2

Answers

6) smoke & stack
7) TEMPORAL
8) HISS
9) 2, 3, 1, 5, 4
10) virulent
11) COMET
12) NORDIC
13) brat & berate
14) veil
15) ANGER
16) cloud
17) CRAB
18) honest
19) REAL & EARL
20) shade

Test 27
1) MIDGE & MIDGET
2) I, O
3) celebrate
4) home
5) SCRUMPTIOUS
6) blister
7) draughts
8) worsen
9) cart & wheel
10) BANJO
11) continuity
12) forge
13) el
14) TYPE
15) late
16) not
17) VRTSGS
18) ALERTED
19) SALIVA
20) LACES

Test 28
1) petals
2) a) 84972
   b) MENACE
3) intend
4) CAMEL & CARAMEL
5) J, L
6) MELTED
7) CURTAIN
8) sent
9) aversion
10) GIBLETS
11) SE
12) CEREAL
13) diesel
14) scruples
15) charm
16) work of
17) WATER
18) solitude
19) PAT
20) TURN or RUNT

Test 29
1) lu
2) pirate
3) try
4) Edmund
5) FIRESTORM
6) row
7) SCRIPT
8) knee
9) Y
10) Simon
11) decrepit
12) DRAWER
13) L

14) phantom & pant
15) park
16) noose
17) water & shed
18) rise
19) blunder
20) pew & crucifix

Test 30
1) precocious & premature
2) CONSTRUCT
3) due
4) BUSH & PLEAS
5) RFLRZ
6) primate
7) bowler & stetson
8) D
9) NEAP, NAPE & PANE
10) 1st, 5th, 9th, 21st
11) BEAK
12) MEANEST
13) XJR, YLQ
14) ot
15) minute
16) RAISE
17) to
18) wrath
19) TH
20) avocado

Test 31
1) ELITE
2) clinic & theatre
3) OCTOPUS
4) referee & umpire
5) JACKAL

88

© 2012 Stephen Curran

Answers

*11+ Verbal Reasoning
Year 5-7 GL & Other
Styles Testbook 2*

6) PRIME
7) PARSNIP & SNIP
8) fox & glove
9) 42 years
10) artiste
11) JOJ, LQH
12) scratch
13) CONCEAL
14) GATE & WREST
15) SEQUINS
16) mute & speechless
17) saw
18) coast
19) yob
20) sword

Test 32
1) SLURPS
2) RABBIT
3) ER
4) 23457
5) P
6) chute
7) 4, 1, 3, 2, 5
8) CATASTROPHE
9) stingy
10) reviews
11) FARMER
12) change
13) POUCH
14) SLOSH
15) dash & board
16) mountain & hillock
17) ENSURE
18) LETS and LEST
19) a) 426573
    b) FEMALE
20) us

Test 33
1) ICONIC
2) case & decrease
3) decaying & fresh
4) ERM, GUQ
5) lizard
6) O
7) hear & ten
8) back
9) sentry
10) stave
11) Pryanka
12) bone
13) microns
14) CAFE & THERM
15) DOCILE
16) KNEAD
17) ponder
18) PARSE
19) ROYAL
20) DETRACT

Test 34
1) TRAIN
2) GLADIATOR
3) WG, DE
4) LE
5) joust & fence
6) frugal
7) LID
8) HUGE & HUNGER
9) AUTUMN
10) badge
11) SITE & TIES
12) panel
13) cajole & coax
14) geese
15) suite

16) bale
17) CREATE
18) a) 93274
    b) BRATS
19) except
20) sand

Test 35
1) tsunami
2) DILATE
3) ZONED
4) CAVALRY
5) susceptible & vulnerable
6) dace
7) ONS, QQW
8) RATION
9) W
10) SALAD
11) a) 428653
    b) TEASE
12) panda
13) fire & storm
14) RID
15) pot
16) righteous & immoral
17) il
18) care & caress
19) TOWER
20) R

Test 36
1) mustard
2) sits
3) TL, OM
4) a) 84573
    b) BLEST

© 2012 Stephen Curran

89

11+ Verbal Reasoning Year 5-7 GL & Other Styles Testbook 2

Answers

5) CEMENT & COMPLETE
6) knife & grain
7) TIE
8) PILL, PILE or PIPE
9) manger
10) timepiece
11) ROCKET
12) certain
13) sadden
14) CARNAGE
15) roach & salmon
16) praise
17) ROBUST
18) edible & credible
19) CATTLEMAN
20) TAIL

Test 37
1) STAINED
2) LMNOP
3) sag & slang
4) CAST
5) Ben
6) protein
7) alien & ate
8) ei
9) rue
10) SAUSAGE
11) service & repair
12) collude & conspire
13) zeal
14) ROBE or BORE or BOER
15) procure
16) tabby
17) ACT
18) OUTLAW
19) trowel
20) T

Test 38
1) APATHY
2) pathetic
3) FLUIDS
4) oil
5) AZG, GBE
6) SCOUR
7) dense
8) bluff
9) jocular
10) R
11) easel & weasel
12) four
13) strike & spray
14) river & bed
15) trusting
16) tableware
17) PLATE
18) salsa
19) early
20) BOND & DEBUT

Test 39
1) precise & prise
2) dealer
3) chew
4) bowling
5) TO, QQ
6) Windermere
7) neglect & treasure
8) SEWING & TANGLED
9) honey & comb
10) ANNOY
11) ir
12) SIXTEEN TIMES
13) thirteen
14) crazy & sane
15) BIT
16) molasses & honey

17) ROAM
18) TERRAPIN
19) produce
20) erratic

Test 40
1) HITCH
2) bravely
3) lash
4) quick & sand
5) remonstrate
6) RE
7) squash
8) CHAT & STEEP
9) see
10) CROQUET
11) IML, LSN
12) TRACING
13) a) STAMEN
    b) 96431
14) races
15) RING
16) violin & oboe
17) scour
18) HEATH
19) magazine
20) bent

© 2012 Stephen Curran

PROGRESS CHARTS

Test	Mark	%
1		
2		
3		
4		
5		
6		
7		
8		
9		
10		
11		
12		
13		
14		
15		
16		
17		
18		
19		
20		

Test	Mark	%
21		
22		
23		
24		
25		
26		
27		
28		
29		
30		
31		
32		
33		
34		
35		
36		
37		
38		
39		
40		

© 2012 Stephen Curran

CERTIFICATE OF ACHIEVEMENT

This certifies

_____

has successfully completed

11+ Verbal Reasoning
Year 5-7 GL & Other Styles
TESTBOOK 2

Overall percentage score achieved _____ %

Comment _____
_____

Signed _____
(teacher/parent/guardian)

Date _____

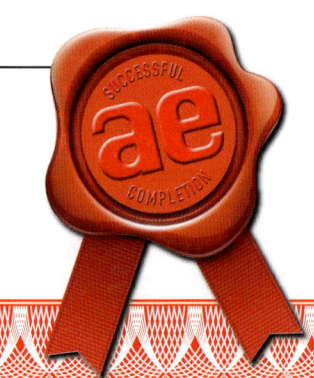